D0976365

ESSENTIALS

of Patents

ISBN: 0-471-25050-3

Printed in the United States of America

10 9 8 7 6 5 4 3 2 1

Contents

About the Authors

Andy Gibbs is the founder and CEO of PatentCafe, the Internet's largest intellectual property network. He has founded seven manufacturing and professional service companies, and is an inventor with 10 issued or pending patents in the automotive, medical device, electronics, sporting goods, methods of business, and software industry segments. His background ranges from garage entrepreneur to Division Executive V.P. for Fortune 500 Mascotech, and from litigation expert witness to venture capital fund advisor.

Mr. Gibbs was appointed by U.S. Secretary of Commerce Donald Evans as a second term member to the U.S. Patent and Trademark Office's Public Patent Advisory Committee, which advises the Patent Office on various matters and reports annually to the President and the Judiciary Committees.

He is a member of the Intellectual Property Owners Association (*www.IPO.org*), the Licensing Executives Society (*www.usa-canada.les.org*), National Association of Patent Practitioners (*www.napp.org*), and the Patent Information Users Group (*www.PIUG.org*). Mr. Gibbs has authored a number of publications and software including: *Boy Scouts of America Drafting Merit Badge Manual, Ironman Inventing, Ironman Business Plan,* and the *PatentCafe Invention Assessment* software program and manual, and has been a contributing editor for *Entrepreneur.com* and *Inventors' Digest.*

As a past Silicon Valley product designer, he has had his hand in the development of many product firsts including: home satellite TV receiver systems, LCD watches, flat screen color CRTs, 3½″ floppy disks, miniature electronics connectors, automotive diagnostic equipment, ink jet printers, UV/ozone water purification systems, manufactured hazardous material storage buildings, and semiconductor testing equipment for companies such as National Semiconductor, Memorex, ADAC Laboratories, ISS Sperry Univac, System Industries, and others.

He is also an accomplished building designer with more than 75 residential, commercial, and industrial architectural projects to his credit including Memorex, Beringer Winery, and Bob's Big Boy Restaurant.

Mr. Gibbs speaks internationally on intellectual property issues, including debates and conferences sponsored by Derwent, UK, and the World Intellectual Property Organization, a United Nations NGO, in Hong Kong and Bulgaria.

His numerous TV and radio appearances as an intellectual property expert include CNN/fn, the Ananda Lewis Show, the Discovery Channel, Morley Safer's American Business Review Series, as well as regional TV and syndicated radio talk shows, and has been quoted by Forbes, Bloomberg Washington Report, Time, National Law Journal, London Financial Times, LA Times, and over 100 other media outlets worldwide.

Mr. Gibbs earned his bachelor's degree in architecture, and master's degree in marketing and business administration. He lives on his Northern California walnut orchard with his software entrepreneur wife Stephanie and two sons. He's an avid cyclist, snowboarder, outdoor sportsman, antique fishing lure collector, and an accomplished woodworker and custom gunbuilder.

You can contact Andy Gibbs via e-mail at CEO@patentcafe.com, or visit the PatentCafe.com Web site (www.PatentCafe.com/corp) for more information.

Sixteen years ago, **Bob DeMatteis** had an idea he wanted to pursue. He pursued that idea, patented it, and today has 20 U.S. patents and 7 pending. Bob owns 16 of those patents—all of which have been licensed and have made money. You can compare his track record to what is reported by the U.S. Patent Office—that only 3 percent of patents ever earn money for the inventor! Sales of Bob's inventions exceed $25 million per year and are used by national giants such as Sears, McDonald's, Walgreens, Kroger, and Subway. You have most likely used some of Bob's innovations at one time or another, when you carry out merchandise in one of the store's printed plastic bags.

Bob is one of the original developers of the plastic grocery sack and is recognized as an innovative leader in the packaging industry. Bob's inventions and patents do not focus on engineering or scientific advances but on making products "people friendly." Bob's newest creations include the M2K plastic square-bottom bag, replacing paper bags in fast-food restaurants, and a new plastic valve bag, the Dry-sak, that is receiving worldwide attention as a replacement for paper cement bags and bulk food bags.

After years of experience as an inventor, Bob had another dream— that is, teaching others how they too can realize their dreams. Bob enjoys teaching just as much as patenting and inventing. From this dream, Bob developed a workshop series, *From Patent to Profit*. These exciting workshops help inventors, innovators, entrepreneurs, businesses, and corporations learn how to patent their ideas and make money on them. His friendly, enthusiastic manner of training gets only rave reviews from participants.

Bob is also the author of the bestseller book, *From Patent to Profit* (rated with five stars at amazon.com). *From Patent to Profit* is based on Bob's years of experience. For first-time inventors this book is one of the most informative, easy-to-read innovation and patenting books available.

Today Bob is an internationally known inventor, author, in-demand speaker, and a certified seminar leader of the American Seminar Leaders Association. He is also a contributor and speaker on inventing and innovating at numerous colleges and universities plus the Small Business Development Centers (SBDC) and the U.S. Patent and Trademark Office and their many depository libraries.

Preface

The book you're reading, *Essentials of Patents,* is about the development, protection, commercial exploitation, and management of patents.

Once the domain of wire-haired inventors, engineers, and their patent attorneys, patents are now at the forefront of corporate value creation and shareholder wealth. The competitive global economy exerts even more pressure on corporations engaged in business internationally.

The rise in counterfeit products and patent infringement cases not only pecks away at the core value of a patent portfolio—it threatens long-term viability of a company's products. In summary, the practice continually erodes shareholder value.

Intangible asset value for technology-based companies has grown from 38 percent of a company's market capitalization in 1982 to 62 percent in 1995,[1] leaving little question as to why so much management emphasis is being put on patents.

Because of the value contribution that patents make to corporate wealth, it's now critical that all managing departments, not just engineering or legal department managers, integrate patent management into their daily routine. Managers generally understand how patents affect the engineering and corporate legal departments, but how do they affect HR, the IT department, marketing, or finance? More important, how can these key managers more effectively manage patents to promote value creation?

In addition to providing the first set of management tools for managers in every department within an enterprise, this book introduces the entire tier of top management to a groundbreaking new quality management program, Patent Quality Management (PQM).[2] By developing a team approach to PQM, every key manager will be drawn into a patent-conscious management style and will be given the tools to effectively contribute to corporate wealth.

Special Note About the 2002–2003 U.S. Patent & Trademark Office 21st Century Strategic Plan

As this book goes to print, the proposed U.S. Patent & Trademark Office 21st Century Strategic Plan remains in limbo. Along with the "fee bill" legislation that would have raised U.S. patent filing fees to new and incredibly exorbitant levels, the 21st Century Strategic Plan was originally slated to go into effect in October 2002. (This follows what appears to be a growing international trend by key patent offices to force the reduction of patent filings through the imposition of very high filing fees. In September 2002, the Japan Patent Office announced plans to increase Japanese patent filing fees between 200 and 300%.)

The fee bill legislation in its proposed form has not gone forward, and provisions of the 21st Century Strategic Plan, including e-government, patent quality, the microentity patentee classification, and more, is waiting in the wings without any confirmed scope or implementation date.

A number of organizations are racing to introduce a replacement bill for the USPTO-offered fee bill, but presently no bill is currently being considered. This will most likely change without much notice.

What this means: Whether a new fee bill goes into effect or not, you can expect a considerable change in the way you currently look at patent management.

Since this book outlines strategic, tactical, and operational considerations for every key corporate staff member, intellectual asset management consultant, and patent law firm, it's critical to understand the huge financial, competitive, and legal impact this proposed legislation will have on every intellectual property owner. It is important for every reader to monitor the near term passage of any fee bill and determine the effects of the bill on operations—it's highly likely that a fee bill would result in a significant increase in patent-related fees (and corporate budget requirements to find patent activity). Understand that if a fee bill does NOT go forward in late 2002 or early 2003, there is a virtual guarantee that patent *pendency* (the period during which a patent status is "pending") will be increased significantly. For most companies in most industries, lengthy delays in patent issuance mean that

- Companies cannot assert patent rights upon an infringing competitor.

- Companies that are required to show proprietary technology to venture capitalists or investors will be unable to do so— possibly for four years or more after patent application filing.

- Fortune 500 / Global 2000 corporations that delay the introduction of new products until patents issue (ensuring defensive and offensive positions) will undoubtedly miss prime market windows in certain industry segments.

In short, during the late 2002 to early 2003 period, we will likely see critical changes to the U.S. patent system that can seriously affect patent

PROPOSED 2003 PATENT OFFICE RULES

Look for text boxes in each chapter that have this title. These text boxes will address potential operational, economic, legal, or strategic impact of the proposed 21st Century Strategic Plan and Fee Bill.

strategy, tactics, and, most importantly, shareholder value. It's critical that you monitor these proposed changes, and change your patent management systems accordingly.

Acknowledgments

This book is a conversation, not a lecture. It's a conversation with and about society's innovation and business leaders. Its message is as old as the exploitative business adventures of Marco Polo, but its methodology is strikingly fresh and smart—made possible only through the insight gained from the experiences of the following individuals to whom we express our gratitude.

Captains of Commerce

For your commitment to capitalism and a global economic vitality, we'd like to thank all CEOs—those Captains of Commerce, along with their ICOs, senior staff and their intellectual property gate keepers. You are the champions with the power to create, protect, and exploit invention and patents while plotting mankind's future. It is because you and your peers have assisted us in creating the underlying patent-centric management process that this book has succeeded in communicating the importance of *patent quality management.*

We'd like to give special thanks to Bradford Friedman, Esq., Director of Intellectual Property, Cadence Design Systems, Inc. for his support in providing his unique views, suggestions, and direction—earned from years "on the inside" as a corporate patent attorney.

Shareholders

For your staunch commitment to fund and support innovation and invention, we would like to thank the millions of shareholders and stakeholders of business. Innovation and prosperity exist in the business world only because you have invested your fortunes in the future of capitalism and American innovation. Patents are quickly becoming the new economy currency, and the concerns that you have voiced to us about patent and intellectual asset management have been a beacon, keeping our focus on reaching out to global business leaders to converse about the important new patent management processes that you expect to protect and grow your investment value.

Civic Leaders

We give special thanks to Under Secretary of Commerce and Director of the USPTO, James Rogan, and Commissioner for Patents, Nicholas Godici, who have embarked on the 21st Century Strategic Plan—a bold initiative to take the Patent Office into the next millennium.

Now, more than any other time in its 200-year history, the Patent Office is walking through a maze of economic, political, technological, e-business, and performance pressures. We acknowledge the tireless efforts of every PTO employee who supports the best patent system in the world—the symbol not only of innovation and capitalism, but also the symbol of one of the most basic human rights: the right to *think, dream,* and *prosper.*

Creators and Innovators

Engineers, scientists, and inventors: you've shared your aspirations and frustrations with us, and you've given us your qualified thoughts on what the "perfect business system" might be in which your creativity could prosper. We know all about the years of challenging yourself to do the impossible. Through experience and follow through, the anticipation of problems and solutions becomes your way of life. You have literally made this world what it is today! With our introduction of *patent quality management,* we've spoken to your business leaders who would nourish, grow, and exploit your desires and expertise to invent and innovate.

Thank you all for helping us to articulate the new business management paradigm: *Essentials of Patents.*

Endnotes

1. Brookings Institute (Washington, D.C., 1999). Study associating "missing value" with intangible asset value.

2. Patent Quality Management System and PQM are trademarks and service marks of Gibbs and DeMatteis.

Introduction

As one of the first important works to define the roles and sculpt the methodology of patent-centric management, *Essentials of Patents* dispels the mystery behind patents. Senior staff members and managers from every department throughout the enterprise organization will take off on a fast-paced educational journey through the convergence of business, law, finance, marketing, operations and, of course, patents.

Patent attorneys know patent law, yet very few can apply their patent knowledge to a specific corporate business strategy.

Chief financial officers (CFOs) routinely involve themselves with mergers and acquisitions, which often requires the valuation of patent portfolios—yet few CFOs know the first thing about patent valuation.

Although marketing managers continue to bet on new products based on market research, few understand the incredible competitive advantage of analyzing a competitor's research and development (R&D) focus via that company's patent activity—yet the information is there for the taking.

In fact, in the hands of knowledgeable, contemporary managers, patent information is becoming a cornerstone of corporate strategy, shareholder value building, and short-term business and legal tactics.

Overlay these trends with the Securities and Exchange Commission (SEC) regulations and shareholder backlash from corporate failures such as Enron and Worldcom, and shareholders are demanding more accountability from the senior staff—accountability to protect and grow their stock value.

In 1776, Adam Smith published *Wealth of Nations*, one of the sparks of the Industrial Revolution that followed—the age of invention and machinery. Smith's economic theory of the principle of the commercial or mercantile system was that "wealth consists in money . . . a popular notion which naturally arises from the double function of money, as the instrument of commerce and as the measure of value."

The fact is, your business is little more than a cog in the new and incredible industrial revolution—the new global economy where *patents* have replaced money. It's nothing short of a new paradigm in economic theory and capitalism. With more than 6 million U.S.-issued patents (and more than 300,000 new patent applications each year), it's clear that the companies that succeed in capturing technology, sustainable competitive advantage, and protected growth will have first secured their fair share of these newly issued patents. Corporate value depends largely on a portfolio of bulletproof patents.

The promise of increased shareholder value drives investment in America's corporations. It's become clear as we entered the new millennium, that nothing has a more profound impact on shareholder value than intangible assets—patents. Those senior managers who are properly managing the company's patents will be tomorrow's corporate leaders. Those managers who are not properly managing patents risk losing shareholder value, will be held accountable, and may be held personally liable by the shareholders and government agencies alike.

As corporate America is reeling from big business collapse, SEC investigations, and questionable accounting practices, chief executive officers (CEOs) and CFOs find themselves now separately reporting the value of the company's patents and intellectual assets—the perfect fuzzy environment for abusive valuation methods, reporting assumptions, and loss of shareholder value.

Although Adam Smith rightfully identified a double function of money as the drive gear in the capitalist machine, he could not have envisioned that patents would become a New Economy currency that would transcend cash and country boundaries.

Today, more than 200 years after the establishment of the U.S. Patent and Trademark Office, the American corporate value owned by shareholders is based more on patents and intangible assets than it is on money and hard assets combined. In fact, the leading, publicly traded high-technology companies can attribute more than 85 percent of their market value to intangible assets—not to facilities, machinery, inventory, or other tangible assets as was the standard just 20 years ago.

In many respects, patents have supplanted money as the primary instrument of commerce, with *more* than a double function that allows the patent owner the right to practice in a monopolistic environment. At the same time, patents are a measure of value.

Patents protect market share for companies, thereby assuming the value equal to the revenue or market, which the patents protect. Patents can live for up to 20 years, so a nominal investment can produce returns for up to two decades. Take a moment to look around your desk—right now. You'll be hard pressed to find an item that was not or is not protected by a patent!

Patents create value by generating licensing fees and royalties. The more progressive companies can realize incredible patent licensing revenue with no incremental increase in capital or assets employed. IBM's licensing royalty earnings were about $1.7 billion in 2001. That's all bottom-line profit.

Patents are routinely used as barter chattel between companies, using cross-license agreements as the mechanism that allows two companies to nonexclusively exploit the patents, intellectual property, and products or services of the other.

In our real world, when one company gets a little greedier than the other, a patent infringement lawsuit can quickly ensue. In fact, more than 2,800 infringement suits are filed in the United States annually— almost 10 every day. Prompting a suit is costly.

Patents are an early indicator of a competitor's strategy—a business barometer by which both business and technical direction can be gleaned by analyzing a competitor's patent activity. Increased patent activity equals increased R&D spending, and that indicates future new product introductions. But what technology and products are competitors pursuing? In the hands of skilled researchers, ever-evolving patent analysis software tools can begin to uncover a competitor's secrets.

Smith's double function of money was a catalyst for the Industrial Revolution, and we suggest with even more boldness (because we have the benefit of experiencing the patent economy) that the New Economy industrial revolution based in patents delivers far more than a double function. Patents function in a very real and potent manner as:

- Market protectors
- Revenue producers
- Value creators
- Employee work incentives
- Competitor monitors
- Barter chattel—tradable on their face
- A measure of value (with SEC reporting under the new FASB rules)

Patents are powerful tools that today must be wielded with executive adeptness. Patents are no longer the byproduct of R&D, and R&D is no longer a department. As business in the twenty-first century unfolds, R&D has become a cross-functional methodology that is now every manager's responsibility.

Patents form the foundation of entirely new enterprises and industries such as biotechnology and the Internet—yet patents are also a liability. The filing of a patent infringement suit by one biotech company against another results in an immediate loss of $65 million in stock value on average.

In order to manage the new money, a shift in enterprise management processes is naturally required. We introduce senior staff and department managers, as well as shareholders who will hold them accountable, to Patent Quality Management, a paradigm of sorts in its own right, as it takes a patent-centric perspective on creating, managing, growing, exploiting, and profiting from patents.

What's at stake? Company value.

And if value drops, who pays? Shareholders!

Essentials of Patents is the focal point that brings together business, money, intellectual property, law, and the management of all these, for the benefit of the shareholder. It is the foundation on which careers, corporations, capitalism, and future value creation is built.

Patent-centric business *is* the new industrial revolution; patents are a new monetary unit; and capitalism is undergoing a patent-driven metamorphosis—to the benefit of the fast, flexible, and focused.

The readers of *Essentials of Patents* are thinkers, strategists, and tomorrow's innovative business leaders who will drive that revolution well into the twenty-first century. Is this you?

CHAPTER 1

Patents: High Stakes, High Value, High Liability

After reading this chapter you will be able to

- Understand what a patent is, what types of patents there are, and how to protect them
- Learn how to file patent applications, including important *new* proposed 2003 Patent Office Rules
- Understand the value of patents to a corporation in terms of shareholder value, market positioning, and licensing revenues

America has a rich history of patents. The U.S. patent system was created in 1790 by an act of President George Washington. His intention was to spur innovation and industrial development in a burgeoning country. Little did he know that he was building the foundation for America's future economic strength. America was destined to become the most dynamic, inventive country in the world. This very patent system, established more than two centuries ago, is the foundation of our country's dynamic prosperity leading into the twenty-first century.

Entire industries have been created based on the granting of patents. Edison, Westinghouse, Singer Sewing Machines, Levi Jeans, and General Electric are only a fraction of those companies that came into existence based on the security of patent protection. Even today, the Pullman brakes used in trains are the original units developed by

Westinghouse more than 100 years ago. Chances are that your company and its jobs can be directly linked back to the creation of new patented products.

Today, new products and new high-performance variations on old ones are being invented. Yesterday's high-volume generic product line has been splintered into many innovative niches. The best way to protect these niches is with patent protection.

Because of their importance to commerce, patents today have more respect than ever before. In the past 15 years, record judgments of $100 million and more—a few approaching the $1 billion mark (*Polaroid Corporation* v. *Eastman Kodak Company,* 16 USPQ2d 1481, 1483 (1990); Polaroid awarded damages of $909,457,567.00)—have been awarded to patent holders as a result of patent infringement suits. In many emerging industries and technologies, patent values have soared 20- to 50-fold in just the past several years. Much of the fluctuation in share value of these companies is linked to the increase or decrease of these patent values.

Simply stated, developing and licensing new patented ideas can be a fast and economical way for companies to protect new product launches, gain new profits, and secure their future. If either you or your company are part of the patent revolution in America, this can be good news for you.

Patent ownership also brings along with it a corresponding liability. There is an old saying that rings true: "Nobody wants a worthless patent, but everyone wants a piece of a valuable patent." This means that valuable patents may be almost as much a liability as they are assets. If your company's patents have particularly high value, chances are they will ultimately wind up in the court system—either used offensively against alleged infringers or in a defensive campaign to prove their novelty and validity.

Patents have become the driving force behind the computer industry and the Internet. Patents protect America's technological revolution,

2

and they can secure our prosperity far into the future. In light of the now infamous Enron meltdown, heated global competition, and changes in world intellectual property policy, the changing business landscape is demanding an ever-higher level of responsibility by corporate managers in every functional department in the organization—a responsibility to manage, develop, and exploit patents to the maximum benefit of the shareholders.

Now it's time for you to learn about patents, the invention process, and how to contribute to Patent Quality Management (PQM). Corporate or outside legal or patent counsel will most likely handle patent legal work for your company, so use this book to familiarize yourself with the terminology, processes, and some of the intricacies of patents. Thus you will be able to more effectively contribute to your company's objectives of creating valuable patents to protect the sales of new product releases and new improvements.

What Is a Patent?

A patent is, in essence, a monopoly granted by the U.S. government to an inventor in exchange for full public disclosure of the invention. When a patent is granted to an inventor, it becomes a public document that fully discloses the details of the invention so that others skilled in the technology can duplicate the results achieved by the patented invention; however, the invention owner retains the sole right to exclude others from making, selling, using, or importing the invention. This concept was so important to America's founding fathers that they made a provision granting rights to inventors in the U.S. Constitution:

> The Congress shall have Power . . . To promote the Progress of Science and useful Arts, by securing for limited Times to Authors and Inventors the exclusive Right to their respective Writings and Discoveries. (United States Constitution: Article 1, Section 8)

Over the decades, the period for which the monopolistic right was granted to an inventor has varied. Today, it is for a period of 20 years from the date the application for patent is filed. At the end of the patent life, the patent owner loses the monopolistic right and the invention falls into the public domain for anyone to make, sell, or import.

Many requirements must be met in order for an engineering development or technical discovery to be considered patentable, but the most fundamental requirements are that the invention is (1) novel, (2) useful, and (3) not obvious to one skilled in the art.

This chapter provides a brief overview to the invention process, but we wish to emphasize the business of invention—that strategic thinking and tactical implementation used by a patent owner to properly exploit an invention for maximized profit and increased shareholder value.

Negative Rights

When a patent is granted by the U.S. government, it gives the inventor the right to exclude others from manufacturing, using, offering for sale, or importing the invention into the United States. In other words, patent ownership does not give the owner the right to make, use, sell, or import the invention, but instead gives the invention owner the right to *exclude* others from practicing these activities for the entire term of the patent.

Patents are sometimes referred to as a legal monopoly because they can be used to prevent others from practicing the invention.

Types of Patents, Duration

There are three basic types of patents:

1. *Utility patents* may be granted to anyone who invents or discovers any new and useful process, machine, article of manufacture, system (or method of use), software and Internet methodologies, composition of matter, or any new, useful improvement thereof.

Utility patents are granted for the term, which begins on the date of the grant and ends 20 years from the date the patent application was first filed.

2. *Design patents* may be granted to anyone who invents a new, original, ornamental design for an article of manufacture. Design patents are granted for a term of 14 years from the date of the grant.

3. *Plant patents* may be granted to anyone who invents or discovers and asexually reproduces any distinct and new variety of plant. Plant patents are granted for the term, which begins on the date of the grant and ends 20 years from the date the patent application was first filed.

Forms of Utility Patent Protection

Most people think of patents in terms of a product, but utility patent protection can take on many other forms. It is important that those individuals, especially those on the PQM team, who have had little previous contact with patents, know these various forms of protection. A heightened awareness to the various forms of patents can help team members identify patenting opportunities, as well as improve the company's ability to protect its product line against infringement.

The language we use to describe the various forms of patent protection is not based on statute, but are general terms used throughout the patent trade, whether that be an inventor, scientist, engineer, patent attorney, or patent examiner. Become familiar with these terms and you and your company's inventive potential will be substantially broadened.

Product Patents

These patents are usually easy to identify because they refer to the physical product itself. For instance, the lightbulb, the paper clip, and the mousetrap are all fairly famous patents. Product patents may also encompass devices, apparatuses, or an entire group of associated products. When a specific unique, novel, useful element is used with a product, that too defines the product as unique and would be considered a product patent. The terms *device patent* or *apparatus patent* are also commonly used, but for ease of explanation, they are best grouped into the single category of *product patents.*

Method of Use or System Patents

These patents usually relate to making products people friendly. They should be of particular interest to every company that sells products in virtually every facet of business. Unfortunately, many companies and their engineers are not familiar with this form of patent protection even though they may be creating superior methodologies and products. Systems patents can also reduce handling time and improve productivity. When you think about productivity, keep in mind the classic economic principle of "productivity produces income." From this perspective, systems patents can be valuable assets to protect the sale of commercial products as well as consumer products. Simply put, systems patents refer to two methodologies:

1. *A method in which a product is used.* For instance, scanning bar codes over laser reading devices. Or, self-opening plastic grocery sacks that automatically open on a dispensing rack when the previous bag is removed from the rack.

2. *A method related to employees' business operations.* For example, a methodology in which machine operators employ computerized statistical process controls to the operation of a piece of equipment. Or, even a method of new employee training that maximizes the time investment.

Both applications save time. They can increase output, improve customer satisfaction, improve quality, increase profits, and so on. Developing superior systems can represent the central focus of a company's product line and result in an endless number of future opportunities as the company strives to make its product line 100 percent automatic and intu-itively people friendly. From this perspective, systems patents can be the single most important asset a company owns.

We know that patents may not be obtained on commonly used products and components, but when they are used in a novel, useful, and unique method, patentability then becomes possible. One or all of the components may be prior art as long as the outcome of the combined use is novel and unique. Think in terms of efficiency, effectiveness, and convenience for the end user, and you're thinking in terms of systems patents.

If your PQM team starts thinking more in terms of systems patents, it will be improving the company's market position and giving the company a competitive edge. Ensuring that all departments understand the importance and the impact of developing and patenting systems, not only for the product line, but also internally within the department, should be a central focus of the PQM team in the twenty-first century.

Process Patents

Process patents generally refer to manufacturing processes. They would typically improve productivity, reduce defects, or offer some value-added quality. These patents are of primary importance to the manufacturing department as well as the engineering department. One of the best examples of a process patent would be U.S. Patent No. 135,245, patented by Louis Pasteur of France, in 1873. It revealed the fundamen-tals of the food sterilization process now known as pasteurization. It is easy to understand the economic impact of such an important process patent.

If the development of internal processes makes a product line so generic with such a narrow focus that it cannot be modified and improved, it will continue to lose market share to those product lines that are more adaptable to change and can satisfy emerging trends.

Process patents can also be a valuable tool to overcome another emerging danger. At times, companies maintain certain manufacturing processes as closely guarded trade secrets; however, if an outside entity files a patent application that covers that trade secret, the company can lose the rights to the trade secret. In other words, the company holding the trade secret would be forced to license its own manufacturing process from the new patent holder, regardless of how long the process had been in prior use. There have been several court case precedents of this kind of action. The negative impact such a scenario could have on the corporation, its management, and the shareholders could be disastrous. The best way to keep this from happening is by filing process patents on your trade secrets before others do. Then you will be in the enviable position of licensing out to them instead.

A shift in focus to being a more customer-driven, innovation-oriented corporation must be accompanied by cost-effective manufacturing processes.

Improvement Patents

The term *improvement patent* may refer to any number of new incremental improvements made to an existing product, system, or process. This can be something as simple as a new tread design for a tire that displaces more water than existing designs or as sophisticated as a method to improve the optical magnification or resolution of the Hubbell Space Telescope.

Improvement patents can also be systems patents, just like the self-opening grocery sack of the late 1980s was an improvement over the prior art "T-shirt bag" invented in 1966. Improvement patents can also be called product patents, if the improvement creates a new, improved product that replaces a prior art product. In a way, it really does not matter how you categorize an improvement patent; what is important is whether your PQM Team takes action when these opportunities arise and you protect these company and shareholder assets with patents.

A customer-oriented company should always be striving to innovate based on customer needs. With total quality management (TQM), making incremental improvements in manufacturing processes of existing products leads to higher quality and improved output. With superior quality, incremental changes in existing processes, systems, and products can then be made to advance the company's profitability as it strives to improve output, sales (via customer satisfaction), and quality. It is simply not acceptable to be complacent with a present market position. If you don't improve your products and processes, your competitors will. If you don't protect them, your competitors will patent them out from underneath you. Ask yourself: Who will be paying royalties to whom in order to stay in business?

Machine Patents

When several elements are used in combination that have some sort of productive output, it is referred to as a *machine patent*. An example is the machine that rolls dough over a mandrel to form a bagel with a round

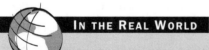
IN THE REAL WORLD

The Right Improvement Can Be the Breakthrough

A well-known fact understood by experienced inventors and product developers is that most breakthrough opportunities are the result of a subsequent improvement patent on an existing product. A new product launch protected by a product patent might get sales started, but a subsequent improvement patent usually creates the breakthrough opportunity—and makes sales soar!

hole in the middle. Or, any number of high-speed bottling machines used in the beverage industry.

Machine patents are usually generated by companies that are in the machinery manufacturing business. These patents often have accompanying process patents. It is also common to include several of the individual inventive aspects of the machinery as part of the overall patented machine. Some people refer to machine patents as *apparatus patents*, thus further blurring the terminology used in the field.

Composition of Matter

Chemical composition patents are scientific by nature, such as those granted for various types of plastics. A burgeoning field of new compositions is in the field of genetic and biological engineering. Composition of matter is sometimes referred to as chemical compositions.

If you are developing new patented compositions, you are probably a scientist working for any number of chemical- or medical-oriented companies or a major university.

Software Patents

This type of patent is more of a catchall term referring to any number of computer- or Internet-related patents. It can include software itself, computer applications such as the one-touch screen, and Internet applications and methods, such as those used for secure credit card transactions.

One of the more famous software patents is the one invented by Xerox that was used by Apple to create its mouse applications. It could be considered an improvement patent as well and was instrumental in turning the PC into a multibillion-dollar breakthrough opportunity. Today, the mouse is one of the standard input devices for all desktop PCs.

One area of concern to companies is software that is developed and used internally for business operations. If the company does not research the concept to verify that it is not subject to an existing patent, the company may be infringing. Or, if the company does not pursue patenting the subject matter—maintaining it either as an internal trade secret or just neglecting to consider patenting—the concept may be subject to someone else's subsequent patent.

Patent Monopoly versus Antitrust

Patent laws were established to grant monopolistic rights to the patent owner. Once a patent issues, the patent owner can prevent others from selling, making, importing, or using a product that infringes that patent.

Conversely, antitrust laws were established to prevent one company from unfairly monopolizing a particular market or industry segment. Antitrust laws conflict in some cases with patent laws. With the growing number of antitrust claims being levied against patent owners (for their electing to "unfairly" shut down infringers rather than license the patent rights to them), this dilemma is becoming a hotly contested issue in the Federal Trade Commission and the U.S. Department of Commerce.

In the past, patent owners have sought to find companies that infringed their invention. After some posturing and negotiation, the result of the skirmish was that the infringing company would usually execute a license to the patent and pay the patent owner an agreed-to royalty against manufacturers' sales. Times are changing. With the recent case of *CSU* v. *Xerox,* it has become clear that a company's assertion of its patent rights, and its refusal to license its patents or technology, does not constitute antitrust.

Nevertheless, the debate continues, and by mid-2002 the Federal Trade Commission (FTC) and the Department of Justice Antitrust Division cosponsored hearings, called "Competition and Intellectual Property Law and Policy in the Knowledge-Based Economy." These hearings included debates ranging from "Patents Should Not Be a

Defense to Antitrust," to "The Monopolistic Right of Patent Owners Is Absolute, and the U.S. Constitution Lays the Groundwork for Patent Owners to Exploit Their Rights," to "The Monopolistic Advantage against Competitors."

So while patents confer monopolistic rights on the patent owner, it is important for key managers and intellectual property counsel to keep an eye on new legislation being developed in the patents versus antitrust arena.

What Is Required for the Granting of a Patent?

In order for the U.S. government to grant a patent, patent laws say that the subject matter must be (1) novel, (2) useful, and (3) not obvious to one skilled in the art.

In retrospect, it's rather easy to identify the usefulness of many inventions: The cost of a pair of Levi's jeans would be outrageous had it not been for Whitney's cotton gin. We take for granted many of the useful features of inventions, such as the improved lightbulb, Velcro, and ZipLoc bags—all of which have proven their usefulness. Products or processes in patent applications that are not provably useful are rejected by the Patent Office. For instance, perpetual motion machines have not been proven to the Patent Office to work and are therefore not patentable.

A patented invention must be *operative*. This means it must work according to the claims in the application. For instance, square tires would be considered neither useful nor operative. A patent on a process whose claims are based on improved output, but that does not perform as indicated, is not valid.

The invention must be *new* or *novel*. An invention cannot be patented if:

- It was previously known or patented in any part of the world at any given time.

12

- It was previously described in an article and published anywhere in the world.

- The difference between your invention and a previous patent (or publicly known product, process, etc.) is such that it would have been obvious to any person skilled in the art. For instance, simply changing size or color for the sake of making your invention different would probably not be patentable.

- It was offered for sale or put into use more than one year prior to filing for a U.S. patent.

TIPS & TECHNIQUES

Think Ahead to First-to-File

The United States is currently the only country in the world using a first-to-invent system. Consequently, there is much international political and legal pressure being put on the United States to convert to a first-to-file patent system. This means that the date and time stamped on the patent application will determine the winner of the footrace to the patent office, and consequently, the rightful inventor.

It is interesting to note that the United States did not always have a first-to-invent patent system. In fact, Alexander Graham Bell is said to have beaten Elisha Gray to the patent office by a mere matter of hours, touching off one of the hottest patent contests of all time, sometimes referred to as the Telephone Patent Conspiracy of 1876.

Now, the United States may be on the verge of returning to a first-to-file patent system. Because this change would considerably alter patent strategy as we now know it, it is important for the reader to remain abreast of any changes to the patent system by occasionally reviewing the U.S. Patent and Trademark Office at *www.uspto.gov,* clicking on "News and Notices."

In this last scenario, the United States (Canada and Mexico, too) has what is referred to as the one-year rule, or the one-year-on-sale bar. It means that the first, true inventor may file a patent application up to one year after the first public disclosure or first public offering of the invention or product for sale.

First to Invent

The United States is the only country in the world that recognizes the rightful inventor to be the one who is first to invent rather than the inventor who is the first to file a patent application. This means that only the first, true inventor will be acknowledged as the patent grantee. Any invention or discovery an inventor is working on that has not been abandoned has precedence over subsequent discoveries that are the same or similar in scope.

If two persons are granted patents on the same subject matter, the inventor who can prove his or her discovery has precedence over the other will have the valid patent. This is true regardless of who filed first or which patent was granted first.

Proof of Inventorship

Three criteria are used to verify legal inventorship:

1. The *date of original conception* may be established by executing an invention disclosure that clearly reveals the inventive matter. This is usually accomplished with drawings depicting the subject matter and adequate specifications explaining how the invention works. Once completed, the disclosure should be signed by a qualified party who can verify the content and the date signed. This would not be a spouse or business partner but a third party who has nothing to gain from the invention's development. Inventor Journals, sometimes called Scientific Journals, are commonly used to establish the date of original conception.

2. Next, the invention must be *reduced to practice*. In other words, it must be shown to work the way you say it works. This is usually

The First-to-File Holds the Senior Position

In the real world it is usually important to file a patent application as soon as possible after conception and reduction to practice in order to protect your rights and the first-to-invent status. The inventor who files first is considered to be in the "senior position" and is more likely to be proven to be the one with the valid patent. The burden of proof is on the inventor who files second, considered the "junior position." It is an uncommon occurrence referred to as *interference,* but the junior position tends to be the more costly position to defend.

accomplished by providing a sufficient explanation in a journal, by producing computer-assisted drafting (CAD) drawings, or by building a functional prototype. If none of these steps is done or documented, then the filing of the patent application is considered the date of reduction to practice.

3. An invention must not have been *abandoned* during its development. If so, it could void the date of original conception and/or the date of reduction to practice. In other words, an inventor must use *diligence* when developing new concepts and inventions.

Filing Patent Applications

Your corporate counsel or patent attorney will be filing most of your patent applications, so this section is more informative than instructive. Several legal and business strategies are involved with the timing and completeness of a patent application, so it is important for all members of the PQM Team to discuss and agree on each new application filed.

U.S. patent applications are applied for in writing to the Commissioner of Patents and Trademarks using one of two types of applications: a provisional patent application or the permanent, nonprovisional patent application. Once either application is received by the U.S. Patent Office, the words *patent pending* or *patent applied for* may be marked on products, brochures, and so on. To use these terms falsely may subject the inventor or individual claiming a pending patent to a substantial fine.

The most commonly used method today to establish that a patent application has been received by the U.S. Patent Office is to send it via Express Mail. The U.S. Postal Service is a U.S. government agency, which effectively acts as a receiving agent for the U.S. Patent Office. Once a patent application is mailed in person using Express Mail Service, it is legally considered received by the Patent Office on the date it was deposited, and the patent-pending notice may be applied.

Nonprovisional Patent Applications

The permanent, nonprovisional application begins the examination process that may lead to the granting of a patent. Some refer to the nonprovisional patent application as a regular patent application. It must at a minimum include the following:

- *Complete specifications,* which is considered a satisfactory description, or explanation, of the invention and at least one claim.

- *Drawings* as required to sufficiently illustrate how the invention works. Photographs are rarely used other than with plant patent applications.

- An *Inventors' Declaration* stating that he or she is the first and sole inventor. If more than one inventor was involved in the creation of the present invention, then all of them will need to execute a declaration.

- The appropriate *filing fee*

Four Step Patent Application Process

The originally proposed 21st Century Strategic Plan put forth a patent process that required four separate steps, outlined here. Although this legislation is not going forward in its proposed form, we've addressed this significant change here in the event a modified program goes forward—it will be important to prepare and change internal processes quickly to take early competitive advantage of these changes.

1 Obtain an outside (third party) patent prior art search from an approved search authority,

2 Make a patent application, and include a filing fee. Thereafter, and within 18 months:

3 File a separate request and include a separate fee for patent examination, and

4 During the 12 months after patent issuance and payment of the issuance fee, the patent will be subject to third party objections (similar to the current reexamination request), allowing parties to challenge the validity of your patent.

Provisional Patent Applications

A provisional patent application, or PPA, is a simplified version of the permanent nonprovisional patent application. Although the name may imply that this is an application for a provisional patent, in fact, the provisional patent application is more accurately described as a provisional application for a patent. The PPA will never turn or mature into a regular patent. The PPA establishes a filing date but does not begin the examination process. It is held by the Patent Office for one year. If it is not followed up with a corresponding permanent nonprovisional application, it is discarded.

The use of provisional applications is becoming more popular because it preserves international filing rights if filed before a first public disclosure. The PPA has some additional strategic and tactical uses, which we will cover in more depth in later chapters. Provisional patent applications must include the following:

- A *cover sheet* identifying the application as a provisional application, the name of the inventor, and other bibliographic data

- At least a partial *specification* that satisfactorily describes the inventive matter, but without the legal claims

- *Drawings* if necessary (they almost always are).

- The required *filing fee*

Who Can File and Who Owns the Patent?

Only the true inventor can own, sell, or assign his or her interest in a patent application or patent. Any individual, firm, corporation, or partnership can own it. An inventor automatically owns his or her patent when granted, unless it is assigned to another entity. The transfer of an inventor's rights is by way of a patent assignment. The assignment of a patent (or application) may be recorded at the U.S. Patent Office, although this is not a legal requirement.

When you work for a company and invent something related to your company's business, on company time and for its use, you cannot ask for compensation for two reasons: (1) your continued employment is considered fair compensation for the invention, and (2) the discovery probably occurred in the job environment and would not have been made otherwise.

If an invention was conceived before joining a company, and it is being pursued and patented for the company's use, asking for compensation from the new employer is a valid request; however, it would be wise to agree upon the compensation before beginning employment and not afterward.

Federal laws state that if you are employed by a firm and receive a patent on an unrelated idea in another field, and development was not on company time or at company expense, your employer cannot claim any rights.

Patents in the Corporation

New ideas usually start out as a conceptual seed from a single person or a small group of individuals, but because patents affect every department in the corporation, sooner or later other managers in the organization will play major roles in the development and commercialization of the patent. One of the foremost opportunities within a corporate structure is the ability to quickly build teams and take on new projects. Fortunately most modern TQM structures can adapt to a team development effort, especially from a top-down directive. The right team can dramatically speed up the time-to-market effort.

IN THE REAL WORLD

Patent Rights Challenged by Antitrust

In 1994 CSU, LLC, a Xerox machine repair service company, filed suit, alleging that Xerox violated the Sherman Antitrust Act, 15 U.S.C. § 2, by monopolizing and attempting to monopolize the market for servicing Xerox copiers and printers. Xerox answered the complaint with counterclaims of their own for patent infringement. The district court threw out CSU's antitrust claims, saying that "Xerox's unilateral refusal to sell or license its patented parts cannot constitute unlawful exclusionary conduct under the antitrust laws."

Corporate structure can be a downfall of some corporations as well. The wrong management style (e.g., autocratic or micromanaged) will have a difficult time fostering a true team effort. If everything hinges on the approval of a single person, it will be slow going.

Of course, patents are considered intangible assets, and under the new Financial Accounting Standards Board (FASB), increased emphasis is being put on financial reporting and patent value as a reportable intangible corporate asset. We cover the financial reporting and valuation aspects of patents in more detail in Chapter 8.

Patents across the Corporate Structure

Patents increasingly contribute to the creation and enhancement of shareholder value, help establish competitive market positioning, and are becoming an important source of licensing revenues. It is no wonder then that managers throughout the organization will increasingly come in contact with patents and will be increasingly required to make management decisions related to patents.

From this position of having provided you with a basic understanding of what patents are, and how they work, *Essentials of Patents* will now lay out the essentials of the business of patents. Patent value doesn't just happen. It is planned (or at least it should be). Patent strategy, patent tactics, and patent management throughout the organization are critical factors in achieving Patent Quality Management.

Patents are powerful tools based on the right to exclude others from manufacturing, using, and selling products that fall under the scope of your patents. Thus patents can be the basis to protect your company's sales and assets. This basis also represents a popular means of generating additional revenue—more specifically, through licensing out your company's patents and licensing in others that may expand your company's sales.

CHAPTER 2

Patent Licensing

After reading this chapter you will be able to

- Understand what licensing is, who drives the endeavor to license, and how licensing can affect a company's bottom line

- Understand the pros and cons, rationale, and basics of licensing in

- Understand the pros and cons, rationale, and basics of licensing out

Licensing appeals to many corporations and can be an attractive means of generating income. To IBM, licensing means $1.7 billion in annual licensing revenue. The term carries similar weight at Stanford University, to the tune of more than $100 million in annual royalty income.

Although licensing is synonymous with revenue, to many other companies licensing means faster time to market or money saved. Whether licensing in, licensing out, or cross-licensing, licensing can create substantial profit opportunities.

The notion of licensing old or forgotten patents in a company's portfolio for significant revenue generation has been popularized in recent books and publications. Although this concept is valid, much of the advice on mining the hidden value of patents through licensing has left more of a hollow feeling in management than it has helped them understand the nuts and bolts of licensing.

This chapter introduces front-line corporate managers to the concept of technology licensing. More important, we'll develop scenarios relating to licensing models as they apply to marketing, R&D, finance, and other functional management groups within your organization. Without the tools to implement intellectual property tactics and strategy at a department level, technology licensing is really little more than a management discussion trend.

Those who would espouse the dusting off of old, unused patents to then extract significant value from them are essentially saying that you can get rich from holding a garage sale of patents that your company has found little value in pursuing. With the exception of finding a valuable

 TIPS & TECHNIQUES

Use the Internet to License Patents

Companies that have technology they would like to license to others need to advertise the availability of licensable patents to others. The Internet is the most efficient, far-reaching medium to broadcast the availability of your technology. The most popular commercial Websites offering general patent licensing listings are:

www.2XFR.com[*]	www.pl-x.com[*]
www.yet2.com	www.patex.com

[*]These sites can provide customized versions for your available-to-license patents and will match the look and feel of your corporate or enterprise Website.

nugget that was simply hidden away, as a management practice, more emphasis needs to be placed on licensing as a proactive process, not a reactive one.

If licensing is a stated corporate objective, however, then purposeful decisions regarding the use of various licensing valuation and Internet patent listing database tools will most likely deliver more consistent licensing revenues in the future or will help you meet your stated objectives.

What Is a License?

A license is an agreement, a contract. A patent conveys rights to its owner, and the owner may use a license agreement to convey those rights to a licensee. The licensee is the receiver of some or all of the rights: the right to manufacture, sell, offer for sale, use, and import products based on the inventive matter claimed in the patent. If your company is the patent owner, it is the licensor, the grantor of the rights. Either party may be an individual, company, corporation, or other legal entity.

Typically, a license is written authorization for a licensee to make, have made, use, sell, and offer for sale products falling under the scope of the claims in a patent. It also sets up the terms and conditions with which the licensee must abide to keep the license in force.

The key terms and conditions of a license typically include the following:

- Payment of royalties
- Maintaining manufacturing and sales records
- Exclusivity provisions (geographic, by industry, technology, distribution channel)
- Marking patent number(s) on products
- Maintaining insurance
- Provisions in the event of the company's sale

- Provisions in the event of bankruptcy
- A time frame

A license agreement may also include details such as:

- Minimum quality standards
- Minimum sales volumes
- Minimum royalty payments
- A right to subcontract
- A right to sublicense
- The use of trademarks, copyrights, and trade secrets

License agreements are tailored to the needs of the organization. They must be carefully written to avoid ambiguity so they are clearly understood by both parties.

Intellectual property (IP) licensing is usually the grant of some form of intellectual property and can be those rights based on trademarks, copyrights, trade secrets, customer lists, and/or patents that are granted or pending. Having a patent granted is not required to execute a license agreement. In many cases, it is even wise to license IP during the patent-pending phase instead of waiting until after it is granted. At times, having a first-to-market advantage can be much more important than the patent itself.

Types of Licenses

Technology licenses come in all sizes and shapes, each one designed to achieve a specific purpose between the licensee and licensor. Some of the licenses that technology managers, corporate counsel, business development, and financial managers routinely deal with include technology transfer agreements, invention licensing or cross-licensing, agreements to licensing in or licensing out, exclusive and nonexclusive licenses, and options to license.

Increased Shareholder Value

The underlying objective to any licensing agreement should be to increase shareholder value. Licenses are used either defensively (as a hedge or counterbalance to infringement claims), mutually (when two companies elect to cross-license respective technologies, usually to the benefit of both companies against a more hostile competitive environment), or offensively (when a patent owner elects to extract revenue from a company infringing its patents, or when a company wants to acquire additional technology).

In all of these cases, the license should ideally result in (1) an increase in revenue, (2) a decrease in loss or risk of loss, or (3) an enhanced market position/market opportunity.

Occasionally, a company may find itself in a situation where it is forced to quickly execute a license—as settlement to litigation, to act on emerging business or market information, or any other variety of factors; however, effective licensing programs are more often planned. They are usually the result of a corporate licensing strategy.

A Drive to License?

Technology licenses do not just happen. With the recent high visibility of the technology licensing trend, it's easy to find literally thousands of pages written on technology licensing. These books and papers explain what licenses are, why licenses are valuable, and some even dig deeply into the theories and intricacies of the valuation of technology being licensed, complete with calculus and statistical valuation methods. Yet others get carried away with the finite legal details, licensing agreement terms and conditions, negotiation tactics, and international considerations.

Unfortunately, most publications lose the original intent, which is to establish a working partnership between licensee and licensor, for the benefit of the shareholder.

IN THE REAL WORLD

License In to Save, License Out to Generate Money

Even low-tech companies can benefit from licensing opportunities. We recently discussed a custom software development project with an enterprise applications development firm. The client company, an agricultural nursery that raised and sold peach, nut, prune, apple, and other orchard trees, engaged the software firm to develop a rather complicated work flow and tree inventory management system. Clearly, the application was unusual, but in its industry, it was not really unique. The client refused to look outside to other orchards throughout the United States for a similar software package it could more easily modify. So, more than two years and $70,000 later, the orchard nursery has its software.

If the client firm had looked at licensing in custom software already deployed at other nurseries, it would have found more than 50 options, including software developed by the U.S. Department of Forestry (free, with only the cost of customization), gardeners' nurseries and, other orchard nurseries throughout the United States and Canada. That's a possible savings of more than $50,000, and more important, the possible savings of 18 months of needless development time.

On the other hand, now that it has its software, will the client nursery look for other nurseries to discuss the licensing out of the software package? Possibly, it could sell a license to other nurseries for $15,000 to $20,000 per location, but the nursery is not interested! Even the information technology (IT) department can boost shareholder value by considering licensing in and licensing out opportunities.

Patent Quality Management and an aggressive approach to licensing could have had a significant positive effect on shareholder value. We're glad we're not shareholders in this company.

Although those concepts reflect current management theory, they preach more than teach and leave middle-level managers barely knowledgeable; therefore, they are ill equipped to identify, construct, and close a licensing program.

Worse yet, the implied objectives encourage the tech transfer managers to seek out that one killer license—the big deal that competitors will talk about for years—whereas PQM challenges every manager to seek out all opportunities, including several smaller, valuable licenses. Incrementally, multiple small licenses provide a more stable revenue foundation, as well as a more defensible portfolio, as compared to a few big winners.

The key element most often not discussed with regard to licensing is: *Who* drives the license—and *how?* We're about to give some common-sense tools to all department managers so they can become effective technology licensing professionals.

Who Drives the License?

Traditionally, technology licenses were driven by corporate counsel and the managers from the engineering or marketing departments. Under a PQM system, the drive to license patents and technology can be expected to originate from the IT, finance, marketing and sales, corporate legal, and manufacturing managers.

Marketing seeks out new sales opportunities, products, and technologies to round out a thinning product line. Finance managers, interested in only half of the technology portfolio of a company they're about to acquire, should embark on a licensing effort to immediately turn the patents they have no desire to use into licensing income, or sell them outright, thus reducing the effective acquisition cost.

Manufacturing managers who discover efficient work flow process improvement software being used by a company in another industry could possibly license a copy of that customized software and realize higher production efficiency for a fraction of the cost of original software development.

If managers begin to look for shortcuts by licensing in proven technology and products, and similarly look for noncompetitive licensees for their own technology, they will have recommendations for the PQM Team to consider at every monthly patent quality meeting.

TIPS & TECHNIQUES

Create a Licensing Plan

The root of any effective licensing strategy is clearly established objectives. Licensing strategy should be driven by a company's desire to achieve one or more of these targeted goals:

- Increase market share.
- Strengthen competitive position.
- Increase manufacturing capacity.
- Reduce production costs.
- Enter into new markets.
- Reduce development costs.
- Shorten time to market.
- Broaden the product line.
- Invest in a matured technology.
- Leverage a small R&D group.
- Defer the bulk of R&D costs until after product sales.
- Strengthen the whole portfolio.

Who Does the License?

Usually a manager can't license a technology alone. In fact, once a patent or technology is identified, the licensing negotiation usually becomes the process to package the license agreement for corporate or patent counsel to sign off on.

Elsewhere in this chapter we outline many of the due diligence points that should be addressed in qualifying a licensable technology. Each manager *can* perform a cursory due diligence analysis on the technology to be acquired and have the presentation ready for the PQM meeting. If the team consensus is a go, the legal department's effort to pull a licensing agreement together will be greatly accelerated and simplified.

Licensing In

Licensing in is the process of licensing the use of patents and technologies developed outside of your corporation to be exploited *within* your organization.

Why License In?

There are a myriad of good reasons why companies should license existing technologies. Most of them are directly related to money—profitability.

As part of a PQM system, every senior manager within a responsible corporation, regardless of size, should pursue licensing in of new ideas and inventions that can augment current product lines, improve output and profitability, lower production costs, and present new market opportunities.

It is a mistake to believe that any company has all the answers to product and technology problems. Nevertheless, we all know a company that we have referred to at one time or another as subscribing to that dangerous affliction referred to as the "not invented here" syndrome (NIH).

When a company believes that it has all the answers, it is setting itself up for competitors to license the best technologies. There are several good examples of this happening in history. For instance, IBM was incredibly slow in responding to the development of the personal computer: a major blunder. Apple Computer took advantage of IBM's reluctance to make inexpensive PCs, capitalizing on IBM's no-show effort. Then Apple Computer refused to license its software to others, which in turn opened the door for Bill Gates and Microsoft to enter the picture.

Hindsight or corporate irresponsibility? Ego or just not knowing? Maybe a little of all and maybe not; however, these examples all show the results of a reluctance to move quickly and license in or license out for a long-term technology or market advantage.

How does licensing measure up in overall operations? Exhibits 2.1 and 2.2 show how dramatically licensing can affect time to market, budget reduction, and earlier revenues. Without a doubt, licensing must be a continuous part of every organization that is committed to building patent-based shareholder value.

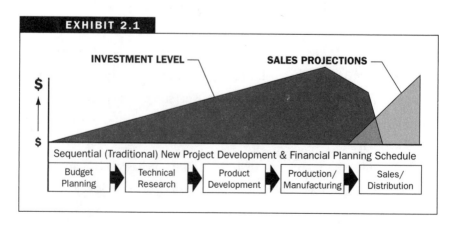

EXHIBIT 2.1

INVESTMENT LEVEL

SALES PROJECTIONS

$

$

Sequential (Traditional) New Project Development & Financial Planning Schedule

Budget Planning → Technical Research → Product Development → Production/ Manufacturing → Sales/ Distribution

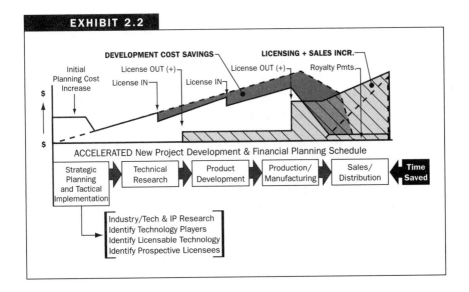

EXHIBIT 2.2

Reduce Startup and R&D Costs

Licensing in can be a welcome alternative to spending hundreds of thousands, even millions of dollars gearing up to go into business. The R&D expense required to develop new technologies usually runs into the millions, and in biotech, that figure runs into the hundreds of millions. The results of these expenditures can be uncertain.

Perhaps the most important advantage of licensing in is the time savings. Being first to market usually carries a greater value than being second or third, as can be illustrated by today's major brand names: Coca-Cola, Hertz, Ford, and so on. Why would you want to wait when an opportunity of magnitude—with first-to-market potential—is presented? In today's competitive business environment, most decisions made by major corporations to not pursue opportunities are based on ego. In other words, the NIH attitude.

On the other hand, many corporations have adopted the principles of an ego-less management system. In other words, doing the right thing for the customer, the corporation, and the shareholder, and not letting personal preferences stand in the way.

31

Defer a Bulk of R&D Costs Until after Product Sales

We've already identified how licensing can reduce R&D costs, as well as accelerate the R&D process, but there is another important financial benefit to licensing in. Royalties are usually paid on the sales of products built on the licensed technology. From a cash flow (and budgeting) perspective, this clearly means that the company will not experience an expense related to the development of the licensed R&D until it begins making sales. In essence, the entire R&D cost is deferred until future product sales are realized.

PROPOSED 2003 PATENT OFFICE RULES

Soaring Patent Fees Support Case for Licensing

Under the 21st Century Strategic Plan, the patent filing and examination fees can easily exceed the legal fees related to the writing and prosecution of the patent. One biotech company randomly assessed a patent application it was preparing to file, hoping to see how the current fees compared to the proposed fees under the 21st Century Plan.

The result was that the proposed U.S. patent fees for this single patent exceeded an incredible $200,000, as compared to less than $5,000 currently. That's more than a 20 times hit to the budget, and no company will be immune from having to consider what technology they can *not* afford to patent.

With soaring costs to patent, it makes more sense than ever to consider licensing in existing technology—at a fraction of the current patent fees. A well-structured license agreement can be as valuable as owning the patent anyway.

Imagine the incredible number of products and technologies that can be developed by a company that is committed to licensing in, even if it is severely cash constrained.

Breakthrough Opportunities

Substantial profit centers are the result of new technologies that are introduced, refined, and matured. It is commonly known throughout the world of invention that major breakthrough opportunities usually occur *after* the first launch, sometimes years later as the product enters the midpoint of its product life cycle. For instance, PC sales didn't sky-rocket until broad-based, third-party software was invented.

Other late-in-the-cycle product refinements have been responsible for breathing new life, or even a dominant market share, into new product generations. By adding fluoride to toothpaste, Crest catapulted into its market-leading position.

In another example, sales of plastic grocery sacks were marginally successful as a competitive alternative to paper sacks, but when the self-opening feature was invented and they could be loaded on to racks, plastic sacks captured the top spot in the 50 billion sacks per year grocery sack industry. Almost regardless of product group, real breakthrough opportunities didn't exist until the product matured and refinements created the breakthrough opportunity.

Market Share Increase

Basic business tenets tell us that during the life of a product, it is important to continually improve its overall quality, performance, and price. By doing so, a corporation may at best pick up additional market share and at worst can prevent market erosion. Because timing is of the essence when increasing market share, licensing in those simple improvement inventions and their accompanying patents can enhance an existing product line quickly, efficiently, and cost effectively.

Perhaps one of the greatest licensing in opportunities exists with well-established companies that have been struggling to maintain market share. One major influencing factor is that the older, well-established companies have a tendency to focus their efforts on the generic product instead of the augmented or potential of the product. They tend to turn away from improvements, other than perhaps the obvious ones, which are usually pursued too late. In doing so, they are playing catch-up, or follow the leader. Thus significant opportunity exists for otherwise defensive-minded companies to license in outside technologies and improve market share.

Strengthen Competitive Position

Manufacturers who have tried to place a few category products into mass retail channels have found out the hard way that major retail buyers are constantly trying to downsize their vendor base. This practice will continue in the foreseeable future.

In order to become a preferred supplier, a complete product line becomes the ticket to large purchase orders and shelf-space domination.

Licensing in can be the ticket to quickly add significant depth and breadth to bolster a thin product line, without the corresponding investment in time and money traditionally required to become a full line supplier. The more products a single supplier can provide to a buyer, the more valuable that supplier is—and the more competitive strength they have in securing their supplier position.

Reduce Production Costs

Licensing in process patents as well as production and training methodologies can reduce production costs. Patented methodologies for reducing waste, downtime, and rework can also make an impact. In mature markets, manufacturing costs becomes the critical factor for survival in the new, burgeoning cash cow market. If technologies are available that others have developed and proved, why not license them in now and take advantage now? Why not slide down the learning curve ahead of your competitors?

Nothing may be more important to the long-term survival of the company than to continually improve its manufacturing processes and reduce costs. This is right at the heart of Quality Management, and frankly, right at the heart of Patent Quality Management.

Expand Product Line

Licensing also represents a simple method of expanding a product line. Corporations may be strong in their core products, but often companies in other fields or industry segments or independent inventors may have viable concepts for new products and profits that will augment the existing product line. Many of these opportunities are relatively easy to launch, too, because they augment the core product group and are often sold to the same customer base.

Invest in an Already Proven Product

Every new product and technology represents some level of investment or engineering risk. Therefore, it stands to reason that one way to reduce (or possibly eliminate) engineering risks is to acquire products and technologies, along with the associated know-how, from a licensor who has proven the functionality, cost, manufacturability, or performance of the product. The added per-piece costs attributable to royalty payments can pale compared to the engineering and performance benefits gained by licensing in a proven technology.

Leverage Your Small Internal Engineering Group

Smaller companies tend to have smaller engineering departments and limited, if any, R&D departments. It goes without saying that massive R&D expenses are out of reach for these firms. Licensing in technologies can turn a small engineering department into a dynamic new product development management group, without adding significant headcount or R&D expense or risk.

Help Fill Plant Capacity

The manufacturing manager can have a significant impact on a company's return on assets (ROA). Nobody knows better than the manufacturing managers that idle machines cost money.

It is a common goal in corporate America to ramp up new products and new product lines to 100 percent output, sometimes referred to as optimum capacity. Unfortunately, this is not a perfect world, and things go wrong. Operating at maximum or optimum capacity is not a realistic approach and in fact could be dangerous because it could create breaks in supply, if something happens. For instance, if a sales department lands a huge order (which should be possible to fill, given optimum output potential) at the same time a manufacturing department runs out of critical part X, the large order may be lost and the company's reputation tarnished in the eyes of the customer. So, the more realistic approach is to have excess capacity in order to ensure a continuous and uninterrupted supply.

Over time, improved production processes can improve output even more and further increase available capacity. In contrast, those plants that continually operate at maximum capacity will have fewer resources available to take advantage of new opportunities.

With extra capacity available, there is very little to lose by licensing in new products to fill that capacity. Frequently, neither major capital expenditures nor an increase in overhead or labor is required. Minor modifications to existing equipment can turn new product production into a new profit center. Such efforts may also improve buying power for raw materials by freeing up budget resources, thus having a positive impact on the balance of the product line.

Also, some employees in manufacturing operations that produce the same product day-in, day-out will be eager to develop new projects and new opportunities. There are always those who will want to take on new projects as a means to climb the corporate ladder.

Avoid Infringement

By licensing in, companies may also avoid infringement. Needless to say, patent infringement can be extremely costly to the infringer. It costs far more to defend a patent infringement case than it does to file one, mostly because the primary defense almost always requires invalidating the infringed patent. The average cost to do this in 2002 was in excess of $1.2 million. Patent holders win about 70 percent of all court cases. If multiple patents are being infringed, the liability of the infringed party is substantially greater. For instance, not only would the cost to invalidate two patents double to $2.4 million, but the odds of winning drop from 30 percent to about 9 percent.

Worse yet, if a company is knowingly infringing a patent, it is referred to as willful infringement. A company found guilty in court of such charges could be liable for treble damages and court costs. In such a case, patent holders would be claiming loss of sales. If the loss of sales reaches millions of dollars per year, the damages for the patent holder could easily be in the tens or even hundreds of millions. Record judgments in recent years have set the stage for patent infringement litigation. If you are the patent holder, this is good news. If you're in the defensive position, it is not.

In consideration of furthering the business of the corporation, to continue to knowingly infringe patents would serve as a potential major breach of trust to the shareholders. Such actions should be avoided at all costs. If your company is involved in such a case, there is a solid argument for saying, "Why fight them when you can join them."

Screening: Due Diligence

Each manager who identifies possible technologies to license should first conduct due diligence before presenting the licensable technology to the PQM Team to review. Due diligence elements that must be considered before licensing in patents or pending patents include the following:

- *Patented or patent pending?* If patents you want to license have been granted, you will be able to determine their scope easily. If they are pending, you will need to review the patent applications and determine if the attainable scope will have adequate protection. The best time to license in new opportunities is usually before the patents are granted so you can be first to market. Waiting until after a patent is granted could jeopardize this position, putting the licensee at a disadvantage to other prior licensees.

- *Breadth of claims scope.* Bulletproof, broad claims make for a valuable technology—one that would be difficult for competitors to design around. Although claims analysis requires the expertise of a patent attorney, managers can perform an initial analysis to determine whether they can design around the patent with ease. If not, it may be a good technology candidate to pursue.

- *Number of claims in the patent and the number of patents.* If licensing a patent with multiple claims (e.g., ones covering the product, certain important improvements, the method of use, and the manufacturing process), the licensed in position is greatly enhanced. This may also be accomplished with multiple patents. Although it may be possible to design around one or more claims of a patent, it becomes exceedingly difficult to design around multiple claims and/or multiple patents.

- *Cost-effectiveness to manufacture.* Price elasticity is invariably a delicate issue with new, improved products. If the cost to manufacture is going to increase, are customers going to be willing to pay more, and how much? If your reason for licensing in is improved profitability, you will want to make sure the product is going to pass this test.

- *Cost to ramp up.* What will it cost to modify existing production machinery to produce the new innovation? Or, will it require new production equipment altogether? In either case, you will need to qualify the return on investment (ROI) in order to justify the project.

- *Attainable, durable market.* Is your company in a position to capitalize on this market, or will it require a completely different or new kind of sales effort? The product will be much easier to launch if it is an adjunct to your existing line, sold to existing customers, by your existing salespeople. If not, does your company have the available resources to market the product? Is the nature of this product a long-term trend or more of a short-term fad? Licensing in usually falls under long-term planning.

- *Exclusive or nonexclusive.* What protection will you have on your investment? In most cases, you will want to ensure profitability and adequate ROI. Will you be able to have an exclusive license on the technology? If exclusivity is not available for the life of the patents, certain other exclusive considerations would be appropriate. We have to keep in mind that exclusive licenses are not always advantageous. Other considerations may include a shorter-term exclusive license allowing you to ramp up and be first to market. This could be as short as one year or as long as three to five years, depending on many factors. Another consideration would be to request a limited number of licensees, providing certain performance and sales benchmarks are met. This limitation tends to help prevent rapid price deterioration and could be as few as two to three licensees over the term of the agreement up to as many as ten.

- *Favored nation status.* It is common to grant the first licensee, the one that is investing the most money and effort to launch a new invention, favored nation status. This would typically reflect an initial exclusive time period to test market and ramp up production and sales. It would also typically include a reduced licensing fee and/or royalty rate. In certain cases, it could also include other elements, such as the right to sublicense.

- *Term of the license agreement.* When licensing in, the term of the agreement should be for the life of the patents. Thus the term will be based on the life of the last of the patent rights licensed. You will need sufficient time to capitalize on long-term objectives. If you will want to trademark this product as well, you will need ample time to establish its presence in the marketplace.

- *Foreign rights.* If you are in a position to market this invention throughout the world and foreign patenting rights have been preserved, can you obtain those foreign rights as well? It may be particularly attractive to a smaller company that has limited international exposure to license a larger entity to drive those sales. In such a case, if the licensor has limited finances, the licensee may opt to pay the foreign filing fees and prosecution costs in exchange for a favorable license agreement and royalty rate.

There are several other considerations as well, such as having sufficient sales volume to justify the investment or knowing that it is a sufficient improvement over existing products and that customers are willing to pay a little bit more. Or is brand loyalty to a competitor strong enough to thwart such an effort? In the latter case, making them want to switch may require pronounced improvements. The royalty rate and licensing fee are also important and can affect the price elasticity in the product's field. Unreasonably high royalty rates or license fees may price the innovation out of the market.

You and your legal counsel will also want to know for certain that licensing in a new technology will not induce the infringement of other patents. Your research must validate this position, and the licensee must warrant it in the license agreement.

Last, if your company is projected out and has simply too much going on at the present time or not enough staff to handle a new project, it may not have the ability to consider any new opportunities.

Licensing Out

Why License Out?

Licensing out should, first and foremost, show that it can generate revenue and profit! Licensing out can enhance your company's portfolio value and increase shareholder worth without any additional investment or sales. At times, this is done by actually sharing in some of the profits of your competitors. Other times, the profits may come from markets outside your company's sphere of influence.

Licensing out your company's technology can also affect the long-term viability of a product line, its long-term stability, and at times, even its ability to survive.

Standardizing an Industry with Your Technology

If there are competing, patented technologies, the one that is made most available to competitors will likely become the industry standard. In other words, the refusal to license out to others can backfire.

There are several good examples of this situation in industry. VHS won out over Beta in the VCR market, even though VHS was inferior. Sony, the developer of Beta, lost out on a windfall of licensing profits by refusing to license to others.

Another more recent example is Apple Computer's refusal to license its software and operating system to others. That decision opened the door to a magnitude of competitors, and worse yet, competing technologies. Apple could not withstand the onslaught of technology being developed by Microsoft, Hewlett Packard, and Compaq. The products these companies developed, commonly referred to as IBM clones, or more appropriately, the PC, prevailed. Apple became the other technology even though it may have been superior.

On the other hand, Xerox Corporation built a multibillion-dollar empire by *not* licensing its plain paper copying technology. Its strategy was to confine all other producers to alternate, inferior technologies that used coated papers. 3M was one of those companies, along with Savin and Ricoh. (Perhaps this was the model that the Sony Beta erroneously followed.) The difference was that Xerox's position was defensible, and they were extremely aggressive marketers. No one had a marketing effort like Xerox. It put soldiers out on the field where none existed before. They won the marketing war by having the bigger army. In contrast, Sony thought that it would monopolize the VCR tape market because it believed that the film industry would select the better technology, but Sony didn't have a marketing plan to support the effort and it failed miserably.

IN THE REAL WORLD

Licensing As a Business Model

Some companies such as Rambus Inc. (Nasdaq: RMBS) have a business model that relies on patent licensing, rather than on the actual manufacturing of a product, for 100 percent of its revenues. Rambus develops and licenses advanced chip connection technology that enables *other* semiconductor manufacturers to produce scalable bandwidth, memory, and application-specific integrated circuit (ASIC) devices. Twenty-five of the world's leading semiconductor manufacturers have licensed Rambus technology, leading to an annual revenue in the $100 million range.

Nevertheless, today the best way to standardize product lines is by licensing out. A small percentage royalty from your competitors is an admirable position to have—one that shareholders will relish as well.

Selecting Licensee Targets

Some target licensees may already be known. They may be friendly competitors, companies in related fields that do not compete with you, or foreign concerns in markets you do not cover. Here are nine elements you can use to evaluate potential licensees:

1. *Quality.* Does this company's present product line represent the same quality as the anticipated licensed product? Patented improvements are usually far superior products requiring superior quality. A Timex-quality watch company is not going to start selling Rolex-quality products any time soon. You want to target those companies that are the right quality fit to license out. This issue may not apply if a new invention can be universally applied to any and every producer, such as Pasteur's pasteurization process. This application would have been irrelevant if it were licensed out to high-end beer and wine companies or everyday milk and cheese product dairies.

2. *Sales philosophy.* If your licensed patents are new product opportunities that require aggressive sales marketing in a market creation sales approach, then your licensee will need to be one that is aggressive, uses offensive sales strategies, and takes advantage of opportunities to create new markets. In contrast to a market creation, if the licensed patents are simple improvements or represent a product line expansion, then partnering with a licensee with a defensive sales strategy may work better; however, companies that have a defensive sales strategy tend to spend most of their effort protecting existing business and market share. They tend to be poor marketers of new concepts and expansion products. Are they aware of this problem? Are they going to be willing to train their sales force? The sales ability of a licensee can be gauged by determining whether it is hungry, offensive, and aggressively looking for new markets to create. If the company is in a defensive mode and is only concerned with picking up addi-

tional market share, this attitude is less likely. It is usually that black and white. With any new product launch or product line extension, the sales philosophy must be positive, eager, and enthusiastic in order to succeed.

3. *Niche or mass marketers.* This point corresponds with sales philosophy. Is the potential licensee experienced in cutting out niches and holding onto them? Is its niche one that is outside your company's marketing sphere of influence? Is it positioned as the progressive industry leader that dominates the niche? Or, is it dominating the niche, losing market share, and hoping to try to get some business back with your invention? This is usually not a good candidate.

4. *Track record.* Qualify some *recent* past successes the licensee has had in either new product launches or product line expansions. Companies that have not had any successes in the last five to ten years or more should be suspect. Not having any recent new product pioneering successes usually says they are satisfied with the status quo. Recent successes suggest that the chances are high that the company will be able to succeed again.

5. *Ability to promote.* Qualifying sales philosophy ties in with the ability to promote. Promotion ability includes preparing marketing aids such as sales brochures and training collateral, advertising expenses, and a tradeshow presence. If a licensee does not have the ability to undertake these efforts with its existing staff, will it hire project managers who can?

6. *Time and people power.* Is the licensee presently burdened with several new projects on the board? Does it have the people resources in its organization to coordinate and guide the project? Can it take the project on right now?

7. *Well connected.* If a licensee is working to create a new market with your invention, is the candidate's sales team well connected at the top-level management of potential customers? Decisions to change are made at the top, not in a buyer's office. Is your licensee also willing to make arrangements to work with end users in test markets to gain the valuable feedback required to perfect the use of the technology in the application?

8. *Finances.* Does it have the resources to launch a new product or to add one on via line extension? Substantial monetary resources

are required, particularly in the early stages of product development.

9. *Total commitment.* If your licensed innovation is a product patent, commitment is an important intangible asset required when launching new products and line extensions. A licensee must make a total commitment to do whatever it takes to get the product on the market. These things don't just happen without significant effort. If your licensed innovation is a new process or system or perhaps business methodology, then it may require nothing more than the licensee's commitment to install it, and for you to make sure it performs correctly. If it doesn't, then chances are they will abandon it later on.

Infringement and Legal Settlements

At times, licensing in and licensing out are instigated by various legal issues, and sometimes litigation. It is hoped that this situation can be avoided in advance.

Although it is desirable to license to others in a friendly manner, lawsuits regarding patent infringement are common. If the corporation's intention has been to license out a technology that is being infringed, then notification and eventually lawsuits are often used as a means to bring about licensing.

When infringement occurs, several considerations will determine your best licensing strategy:

- *Your technology development strategy.* Are you planning on developing, manufacturing, and marketing the technology yourself or is licensing out your intention?

- *The size of the infringing company and how many companies are infringing.* There will be a different strategy if there are a few small infringing companies as opposed to one or two large ones. When pursuing infringement litigation, finances have to be considered. At times, settling with smaller companies infringing your technology can be a much more cost-effective

45

approach than getting embroiled in an expensive battle with a large entity and its huge bankroll.

- *Your patent's scope and integrity.* Are the claims being infringed bulletproof? Is the infringement literal, or does it fall under the Doctrine of Equivalents? The Doctrine of Equivalents states that if an infringing element "operates in substantially the same manner, by substantially the same means, and produces substantially the same result, it infringes." Literal infringement, supported by close scrutiny of a patent examiner during prosecution, is the best position to have.

- *How much money is involved?* Is the infringement of minor or major consequences? Does it represent annual sales of $20,000 or $20 million? This is important to know if consideration of a potential suit includes lost sales. Also, the statute of limitations is six years. After several years, the amount of infringed sales may be substantial, making it more worthwhile to take action. Likewise, if the infringing company is now well established in the marketplace, it is more worthwhile for the company to settle promptly. Last, if the infringing party had been put on notice for patent infringement several years ago, then it could be liable for treble damages. This could become a grave situation for company officers and shareholders alike.

- *The financial condition of infringers.* Are the infringing companies able to defend themselves? Will they prefer to settle quickly in order to avoid expensive litigation? Keep in mind that the cost to invalidate a patent is usually about $1.2 million or more.

- *Your financial condition.* Is the corporation able to afford patent infringement litigation? If not, is legal counsel willing to represent the case on a contingency basis? Providing that the scope and integrity of your patent are adequate, and the amount being infringed is substantial, finding contingency attorneys should not be difficult. With the potential of a substantial payback and with the greater percentage of patent infringement awards being ruled in favor of the patent holder, many legal entities are willing to take on cases with such favorable odds.

Keep in mind that patent infringement is not necessarily bad news. It often has a very positive outcome and, as already mentioned, it can even be a gold mine for licensing revenue.

Packaging for License

When product developers design new products, they do so with the customer in mind. All of the product's features and benefits are intended to fit the demands and desires of the market that the product is intended to serve.

Preparing a technology to be licensed out requires no less care. Over the past few years, we have seen an incredible rush of companies that will help patent owners list their technologies for license, with dismally poor results. The reason for the failure of technology transfer market-places to create deal flow, or sales, is that the technologies are all stuffed into a database with incredibly poor search capability. The analogy to trying to find a licensable technology in a disorganized data structure is trying to find lightbulbs in a Wal-Mart store with paint, housewares, stationery supplies, soda, tools, shoes, and children's clothes all stuffed on the same rack.

Packaging a technology for license requires taking care in the following tasks:

- Describing the technology using terminology the *licensee* would be expected to use when searching and considering the license

- Incorporating key points that help articulate the value of a technology. These points may include the fact that the patent has survived infringement challenges and has several derivative patents (continuations in part, divisional patents, and so forth).

- Describing the market or product applications for a particular technology. Listing the technology itself without any real

application notes does little to assist the licensee in understanding how that technology can be of any benefit to its
product development or sales efforts.

- Creating a clean, easy-to-navigate Web site that will act as a
  24-hour sales agent. A great example of such a Website is
  General Electric's technology transfer site at
  www.GEPatents.com.

- Licensing in a branded technology exchange. Patent Exchange
  Web sites, such as *www.2XFR.com/branded.asp*, incorporate the
  best tech exchange tools, and a logical and searchable data
  structure, into a corporation's Web site look and feel for a fraction of the cost of developing and maintaining one's own
  online technology exchange.

Cross-Licensing

The American style of a competitive business environment is being
slowly augmented by cooperation. Cooperative business developments
are commonplace throughout most of the world but are somewhat foreign to the American way of business. Cross-licensing dovetails perfectly
with cooperative efforts. Frankly, it usually makes sense from a competitive point of view as well. First, it is improbable that a single corporation
or entity in a given field will invent all the best technologies and all the
best products; its competitors will tend to develop other concepts that
may be of great value as well. With patented technologies covering various aspects of an invention, you have the making of a cross-licensing
relationship, which is to the advantage of both parties.

CHAPTER 3

Patent Strategy

After reading this chapter you will be able to

- Understand the importance of developing a patent strategy, including development, protection, and exploitation
- Establish the goals and objectives of a corporate patent strategy
- Understand the mechanics of a provisional patent application (PPA)
- Understand the mechanics of a Joint Development Agreement (JDA)
- Understand the process of patent searching

Corporate patent strategy begins with the big picture. Fundamentally, the patent strategy sets the stage for how the patent owner will develop, protect, and exploit patents. More specifically, patent strategy may include the following: protecting the present product line, protecting market share, product line extension, new product opportunities, licensing out, portfolio expansion, and building shareholder value. Patent strategy is the overriding mechanism that helps direct investment, resource allocation, expectations, and policy development within an organization. Strategy helps define the tactical operations intended to maximize patent value.

The Importance of Having a Patent Strategy

When a PQM team plans the formation of its patent strategy, many issues will be addressed. Patent strategy is no longer just for engineers and attorneys. The perspectives and participation of corporate marketing, information technology, sales, engineering, human resources (HR), manufacturing, and legal are *all* important to crafting a solid patent strategy. Some of the business, legal, and financial considerations that go into the strategy discussion include when a company should or should not file a patent, how many patents should be filed, financial objectives and budget limitations, competitive positioning that should result from the patent plan, patent licensing strategy, strategy guiding the filing of patents in foreign countries, long-term revenue objectives, and much more.

There are so many different strategies (and tactics) related to the management of patents, it's almost as challenging as an international war game, but patent development and management is anything but a game.

Generally speaking, there are four corporate strategies in use today: (1) the castle and the moat theory, (2) patent the tree, cut the forest, (3) the shotgun approach, and (4) patent as you go. Once a company centers on a particular strategic theme, it can begin to develop a more sophisticated approach to many of the details that may overlap.

The Castle and the Moat Theory

What this means is that the corporation builds a castle of technology, protected by a moat of patents. This is a perfect strategy for a well-financed startup company or new product opportunity within an existing corporate structure. The objective is to patent every aspect of the new opportunity. Typically this includes the product, the various individual attributes of the product, the various methods of use it may have, the processes and the machinery used to make the product, and at times the compositions used as well. With software and Internet applications, the strategy may include not only software-related patents, but also copyrights and trademarks. An example of a company employing the castle and moat strategy is Gemstar-TV Guide International Inc. (NASDAQ: GMST), which holds 200 patents on technology it believes will be the core for the convergence of interactive television, Internet, and computers. Competitor iSurfTV has 80 patents pending and has burned through more than $10 million in venture funding in an attempt to build its own technology castle.

Although it may be possible to design around a single claim in a given patent, it becomes exceedingly difficult to design around a multitude of claims in multiple patents. This approach is sometimes referred to as Cobras in a box. A person may reach inside without getting bitten, but sooner or later, one or more of those snakes will strike!

Patent the Tree, Cut the Forest

Frequently, a company will not have the unlimited patent budget to patent every invention in every country. In such cases, the company will spend more time deciding what *not* to patent rather than what it *will* patent.

The danger in not patenting a core technology is that a competitor may patent the discovery in the future and bar the original inventor from practicing the invention. In other words, if you don't patent your invention, someone else may.

One method to prevent other companies from patenting your technology even though you elect not to has been used successfully by IBM over the past decade: Pick the biggest, strongest tree in the forest (your core invention) and patent it. Next, cut down all of the other trees in the forest so only your strong one is left standing. In other words, publicly publish a defensive disclosure for each and every other concept, derivative technology, alternate embodiments, and engineering notes so that no other company will be able to patent a technology close to your core technology. Put simply: If you can't patent it, nobody else will either. Once all other possible methods or technologies have been published, they will serve as prior art to dissuade other inventors and inventions from patenting.

IBM, Hewlett Packard, and Xerox are a few examples of companies that have built their own online technical bulletin repository. Although some do-it-yourself publishing may satisfy the legal test for proper technical format and disclosure, most companies seeking this affordable strategy do not have the investment necessary to build a huge technical disclosure database. In lieu of trying to build your own disclosures program, consider using *www.IP.com,* a relatively new company that will publish your technical disclosures for about $100 per document. Compared to the $10,000 average patent cost, this method is a cost-effective strategy.

The Shotgun Approach

Large, well-financed R&D departments may take this approach. They believe that if just one of many patents is a big hit, that will justify the strategy. Generally speaking, this is true. Mobil Chemical's polyethylene packaging division had this philosophy in the 1970s and 1980s. They filed dozens of patents on plastic grocery sacks and systems, most of which were innocuous, either easy to design around or of little commercial value; however, one of its patents on the subject matter of "stress-relief notches" used on plastic grocery sacks became a standard manufacturing attribute used in the entire industry. Stress-relief notches were an important feature on thin-gauged plastic sacks, which could otherwise break at the base of the handle if not used. Mobil's licensing and subsequent litigation on the infringement of the patent paid off big time, with earnings in the hundreds of millions.

Problems associated with the shotgun approach are obvious. It requires a lot of financial resources, smart inventive people, and luck.

This approach has lost popularity as corporations have begun focusing more on specific targets and more definitive results for their investment and efforts.

Patent As You Go

This is perhaps the most commonly used approach by small- and medium-sized corporations. It is usually used to protect various aspects of their product line as they are created and evolve. It is easier to control costs with this approach, and if the corporation's market is solely the United States or North America, there are several viable strategies and tactics it can use.

PROPOSED 2003 PATENT OFFICE RULES

Huge Impact to Patent Budgets

At the time of this writing, patent fees and legislation under the 21st Century Strategic Plan are yet to be finalized; however, the new rules and fees (effective October 2002) are sure to turn patent strategy upside down.

Budgets will be hardest hit under the new rules, with the patent office fees related to filing a single patent increasing by $10,000 in some cases (not including patent attorney fees). This change will force companies to reduce the number of patents they file.

This fee escalation can put patent licensing high on the list of strategic objectives. If an issued patent can be licensed in from the inventor for little or nothing in advance, then the patent acquisition costs to the company can plummet, possibly even lower than before the new fee structure went into effect.

Have patent counsel review the final 21st Century Strategic Plan rules and recommend the necessary changes to your corporate patent strategy.

Establishing Goals and Objectives

Team Effort

The corporate patent strategy pervades the PQM system of the corporation. It sets up the tenets for a team effort among the departments that results in quality patents. The PQM system is therefore the means you use to fulfill corporate patent objectives.

Nothing may be more important than using the team approach to creating, inventing, and qualifying new opportunities with the corporation. This includes new product launches, improvements to existing products, new methods and processes in manufacturing, and license in or license out opportunities. Swift communication among the departments can quickly qualify whether changes, improvements, and new processes will have the desired outcome and help determine the best approach to solving certain problems and which ones should be pursued or abandoned.

A team effort saves vast amounts of time and monetary resources. In today's business climate, being fast, flexible, and focused is paramount to success. There is no better way to propel inventive efforts forward than through a team effort.

Granted, most new concepts start out as a spark, a creation from a single individual, but turning that initial spark into a patentable concept requires a team effort. All individuals in all departments of the corporation should have the ability to suggest and propose new inventive concepts. New products are no longer the sole responsibility of a product development group. Manufacturing improvements are no longer confined to engineering. After all, product developers are not marketers and engineers are not machinery operators, yet each can contribute valuable improvements to the technology that are unique to their skill set and field of expertise. All of these improvement contributions constitute PQM.

Once concepts are introduced by individuals at the department level, they can be quickly cross-evaluated through other departments, and the best concepts can be assessed and pursued. The PQM system establishes the departmental teams and the cross-evaluation methodology. Fortunately, a new PQM system can piggyback onto an existing TQM system. Thus it can become effective in a relatively short time frame and start generating results promptly.

Patents Provide a Competitive Edge

Whether you are launching a new technology or product, protecting or expanding an existing product line, or taking it into the future by creating the next generation, patents can provide a competitive edge. Putting competition at a disadvantage with inferior products, or alternate technologies, is a wise corporate patent strategy. This approach goes right to the heart of the competitive business environment in America.

Increase Shareholder Worth

Corporate responsibility includes an obligation to shareholders to increase their worth. This can be accomplished with patents in three ways: (1) they can provide additional profits in the corporation with product sales; (2) they can be licensed out and generate additional corporate income—a model that generates more than $1.7 billion in licensing revenues each year for IBM; and (3) the new-for-2002 Financial Accounting Standards Board (FASB) Rule 142 has reset the stage for how companies account for their intangible assets, giving the CFO the opportunity to categorize and report a growing patent portfolio with a rather direct impact on shareholder value.

Increase Product Life Cycle

A product's life cycle is increased by patent protection in two primary ways: (1) having patent protection on the basic product means you automatically have some control over its life cycle potential; and (2) by being in control of the product's future, ample opportunities should arise to create new improvements, which can be patented, thus further extending product life.

An excellent example is Zip-Loc bags. In the mid 1960s, the original concept was invented and patented. It incorporated a single male/female rail for closure. The company built up its market over the course of the next 12 to 15 years. It stopped import knockoffs from entering the United States and generally had its way in the marketplace. In the late 1970s, the importers were preparing a major onslaught into the U.S. marketplace with inexpensive Zip-Loc–style clones. Just about this time, though, Zip-Loc introduced its double-rail version, which was far easier to close than the original single-rail version. The outcome? No one wanted the single-rail version, when the easy-to-close double-rail version was about the same price. The result is that Zip-Loc extended the product life for another 17 years (the time duration of patents in the late 1970s). It was not until 1992 that Zip-Loc sold its double-rail patent with only three years left on it to Dow, along with its trademark, Zip-Loc, for $54 million. It's easy to see that the patents dramatically affected product life cycle and served as protection to establish the Zip-Loc trademark as the leading brand. The sale to Dow was a good deal for both parties at the time. Today, it seems like a bargain price.

Domestic and International Protection

Another consideration in strategy is whether to file international patent applications. Two important considerations for the corporation are its international marketing exposure and the expected sales volume of the patent products. Obviously, a company with a strong international sales presence and a product with substantial international sales potential is worth pursuing. The only requirement is whether the company has sufficient financial resources because the process can be costly.

Many new inventions may not have strong sales potential overseas. If this is the case, the high cost of patenting in foreign countries has to be weighed against sales potential. We have to remember that the United States is roughly 30 percent of the world economy and the country in which it is most important to have patent protection.

If a corporation does not have good international sales coverage, it may elect not to pursue overseas patenting. It may take an alternate approach by seeking out overseas partners that may be interested in developing those markets. These partners can pay for the cost of patenting in their respective countries. In exchange for this investment, the patented technology could be licensed out to the foreign partners on an exclusive or limited exclusive basis in their marketing region.

Defensive Patents

At times, it may be valuable for the corporation to patent alternate technologies that may conflict with the corporation's present product line or present technological developments. This may include technologies considered second best, or inferior, to the present technology. This may also include superior technologies that pose a threat to present technology in which the corporation has invested heavily.

Policy Set by Committee

Strategy is not set by a single individual but must be set by the PQM Team after careful consideration and input from all departments. The strategy that will be pursued must consider finances, present and future sales position and opportunities, engineering ability to develop new improvements and new products, and of course the human resources to execute the planned strategy. Unlike the tongue-in-cheek references to management by committee, PQM requires the technical, financial, marketing, and legal expertise represented by the PQM Team.

Using the First-to-Invent Patent System

NOTE: At the time this edition was published, there were legislative rumblings and activist movements to change the U.S. patent system from a first-to-invent to a first-to-file system. It is important for the chief legal officer or patent counsel to keep the PQM Team informed of changes to the current first-to-invent system because this will have a significant impact on patent strategy if the laws change.

Entities in the United States can use the first-to-invent laws to their advantage when developing new concepts. Many inventors, product developers, and engineers in the corporation have applied this important law through the years.

First-to-invent laws provide the ability to develop a technology on a confidential basis without losing patent filing rights. As long as the inventive matter is kept confidential before filing a patent application, provisional or nonprovisional, then worldwide filing rights are also preserved.

New technologies may take several months, or even years, to develop and become truly understood. During this period, various approaches may be tested and abandoned and the more efficacious ones pursued. A chief benefit of using first-to-invent laws to your advantage is the preservation of time and money. If patent applications were filed on all the various approaches that were tested and later abandoned, a time-consuming, expensive effort would result. The pursuit of filing applications on abandoned technologies would result in a series of worthless or abandoned patents. By using first-to-invent laws to your advantage, patent applications can be filed on only the efficacious technologies and not on the inferior ones.

Recordkeeping

To use first-to-invent laws to your advantage requires excellent record-keeping methods, including verification of the records and a supporting paper trail. Recordkeeping is best accomplished by using a daily log such as an inventor's journal, also referred to as a scientific journal. Don't let the tech-sounding name of this tool imply that journals are used only by engineers. In fact, marketing, financial, IT, HR, and manufacturing managers should be required to keep journals as well.

Recordkeeping in a daily log typically starts with the original invention disclosure that establishes the date of original conception and then subsequent documentation showing how the invention is reduced to practice. Depending on the corporate PQM policy, these logs require a verifying signature of the subject matter on a regular schedule. This schedule could be daily, weekly, or as required.

In addition to maintaining daily logs and records, all drawings, prototypes, materials lists, product testing results, and surveys should be kept in order to maintain a continuous paper trail. Regardless of corporate strategy, it is wise to maintain these records in a secure archive in case they are required later. A secure archive may be considered metal fireproof containers, at times safes, or at the very least, cardboard boxes that are properly stored. Producing such documents as may be required at a later date can result in avoiding costly litigation and interference proceedings.

Using the One-Year-On-Sale Bar to Your Advantage

If a technology being developed is not going to be exploited worldwide, the one-year-on-sale bar, more commonly called the one-year rule, can be used to postpone the costs associated with filing patent applications. This strategy may also provide time to qualify the inventive matter in test markets for up to one year. Once a product or its subject matter has been publicly disclosed and offered for sale, then international filing rights are sacrificed, but patent filing in North America—the United States, Canada, and Mexico—will have been preserved, providing a patent application is filed before the end of one year after the initial public disclosure.

In addition, there are times when a new improvement is made to an existing product that is not believed to be substantial, but some months after the product's launch the improvement turns out to be of importance. The one-year rule can be applied and one or more patent applications may be filed within that first year of disclosure to protect it. The one-year rule can play an important part of patent strategy.

Using Provisional Applications

Greatly simplified, faster, and easier to write, the provisional patent application (PPA) is becoming a valuable tool. It may be used as an intermediate step either to put others on notice with a patent-pending message or to preserve international filing rights. The key advantage is the speed of filing such an application. Usually the most time-consuming elements in filing the permanent, nonprovisional application are the legal claims. These are almost always written by the corporation's general counsel. By filing a PPA, as much as a few weeks or months can be saved. A PPA sets a priority date, preserves all patent rights, and often gives the patent attorney additional time to write claims.

The permanent, nonprovisional application is then filed up to one year later. There are several advantages to waiting: (1) it keeps the inventive matter confidential because it is not subject to publication laws; (2) it helps spread out costs by delaying the greater expense of the nonprovisional application by up to one year; (3) it enables the developer to thoroughly test the marketing arena; and (4) it gives the ability to continue to develop alternate technologies based on market acceptance, or rejection, as the case may be.

If the intention is to solely post patent-pending messages with the intention of perhaps abandoning the applications later, or if the inventive matter is relatively narrow, the strategy of filing a PPA first followed up by the nonprovisional application later stretches out the patent-pending period. This is not a particularly valid position to be in, but nevertheless, it is a strategy used on rare occasion. If the current U.S. first-to-invent system changes to a first-to-file patent system, the PPA may be the most affordable way to quickly put a patent application on file first.

Alternately, because the costs of filing a provisional application are low, the tactic of filing PPAs on *all* technology developments is becoming popular with some larger companies. The thought is that during the 12 months while the PPA is pending, the company can elect which filings it wants to pursue with regular patent applications and which PPAs it wants to abandon as publicly disclosed prior art. This is an alternate strategy to publishing a technology disclosure because, unlike the defensive disclosure publication, which cannot be called back after publishing, the PPA buys up to one full year for the PQM Team to determine the best approach for each patent application.

PPAs and Product Development Strategy

One patent strategy you can use to coincide with new product development is to file PPAs whenever new discoveries are made. This can be a particularly cost-effective approach when multiple discoveries are being made but it is unknown how they will ultimately pan out. It can also be an effective strategy to use when you are pursuing a single product improvement innovation.

We know that new product developments tend to go through a metamorphosis as they are developed and tested. There are usually several features, elements, and processes to qualify, resulting in numerous discoveries and qualification of the discoveries. Typically, this process is accomplished through interdepartmental review or through product testing. Qualifying inventive matter takes time because prototypes need to be made and then tested, first in-house and then later by unbiased parties. During testing, it is common to discover functional problems with the new product, resulting in improvement, modification, or at times complete abandonment.

Because PPAs are a simplified version of the permanent patent application, they can be prepared much faster and at less cost. Filing fees are less than $200 and attorney's fees to draft are far less than the permanent application because claims are not required. If a PPA is filed on new discoveries before and during the qualification and testing process, priority dates are promptly established. If, during qualification and testing, a particular feature or element does not work as anticipated, or requires redesign, there is not much lost if a PPA has to be abandoned. Likewise, it then becomes a simple task to file a new PPA on the new inventive matter or any new improvements made or discovered.

Your strategy may then be to combine several PPAs into one or a few permanent patent applications or to keep them separate and file individually. In the United States, it is easier to file patent applications with multiple inventive matters that will be split out into a divisional patent by the patent examiner. In the international community, however, patent filings tend to be more specific and the applications are not

TIPS & TECHNIQUES

Patent Pending Is a Warning

A beneficial deterrent of filing multiple PPAs is the ability to announce "Patents Pending" on your new product launches. For instance, if you have filed seven PPAs, you can mark the products with the language, "7 U.S. Patents Pending." This shows serious intent and effectively gives warning to the industry that you expect several patents to issue.

split out. Thus, filing discrete applications on individual PPAs may be your best ploy.

Many inventive opportunities arise out of improving a present product or process. Typically this begins by identifying an existing problem, then pursuing development for a few ways to possibly solve it. Usually the best single means to solve a problem is pursued and tested. Filing a PPA early on protects the priority filing date and can speed up product testing. It would allow the improvement to be publicly disclosed to test and confirm functionality and customer acceptance, without sacrificing international filing rights.

During testing, inventive solutions often do not function as anticipated or turn out to be too costly. Thus abandoning a useless PPA is not a major ordeal. New PPAs can be filed to protect the subsequent solutions that are then quickly developed.

Joint Development Agreements

A means of developing new products and opportunities that is growing in popularity is partnering with a Joint Development Agreement (JDA). If your company plans to attract JDA partners, you'd better have something to protect.

A JDA partner may be a raw materials supplier looking to expand sales, such as a major plastic resin supplier who sees an opportunity to

IN THE REAL WORLD

Patent As You Go

It is rarely the first patent that makes a company a lot of money, but instead some later improvement that becomes the breakthrough opportunity. It would be a travesty to not have patented those simple improvements!

convert a paper product line. It may include expansion-minded sub-contractors who manufacture goods for you or an international marketing entity that desires to expand your domestic sales throughout the world.

There are tremendous benefits to having JDA partners when developing your new innovations. They can play a major role in preserving cash flow. They may contribute to your R&D effort by providing raw material specifications, cost-effective manufacturing processes, marketing data, news releases, or even sales contacts. With the right JDA partners, a new innovation may quickly rise to prominence, whereas it may otherwise flounder or slowly ramp up over several years.

Patent protection is crucial for JDA consideration. Your ability to partner depends on the scope of your patent protection. It would be uncommon, if not unheard of, to partner without some form of protection—patent protection being the primary source. JDA partners typically want to see substantial patent protection available in the sphere of their marketplace, either domestic or throughout the world. This usually means multiple patents, or patents pending, covering the new innovation, whether it's a product, a method of use, or a manufacturing process.

Issued patents may not be required, and in fact, experienced, competent researchers and IT personnel can generally spot a new opportunity and qualify the scope of the inventive matter with or without a patent issued. Why would you or a JDA partner want to wait for patents to issue if there is an immediate opportunity now? It makes no sense. The JDA partners who are willing—in fact, eager—to enter into a development partnership with your innovative company know that you can't wait to bet on a horse until after it races. Aggressive JDA partners will search out new opportunities and be willing to invest their time and money now.

Using Nonprovisional Patent Applications

Nonprovisional patent applications may be filed with or without first filing a corresponding provisional application. At times, there are advantages to filing the nonprovisional application first.

If the developing technology is believed to have a short lifespan, such as software, it may be wise to file the permanent, nonprovisional application at the earliest convenience. Nonprovisional patent applications are then reviewed by a patent office examiner, and a patent may be granted accordingly. It makes little sense to begin with a provisional application, which is not reviewed by the U.S. Patent Office, followed up by a nonprovisional application and thereby delay the granting of a patent.

If a new product or technology has been introduced to the marketplace with or without the filing of a provisional application, and a competitor begins producing a similar product that will infringe on the eventual claims of the patent, then the immediate filing of the permanent, nonprovisional application would be desirable.

Using PCT Applications

The Patent Cooperation Treaty (PCT) covers most developed countries in the world. There are two chief times that the filing of a PCT application may precede that of the filing of the standard nonprovisional application:

1. If the technology is going to have a more immediate impact on overseas sales, then filing a PCT first may make sense. In this way, those countries of most importance, or even the entire world, can be designated.

2. As a financial maneuver, a PCT can be filed as a money management tool. The PCT permits filing an international patent application either immediately or within one year of filing a patent application in any of the member nations. The PCT process therefore delays the deadline for payment of more expensive filing fees in foreign countries for up to one year and a half beyond

the time in which foreign patent filing would have otherwise taken place.

Patent Searching

Patent searching, if applied correctly, can be a powerful business and engineering development process. Through patent searching, one can achieve the following:

- Determine whether a new invention is novel and warrants further development investment.
- Identify a competitor's technology development trend, and possibly ascertain a relative level in R&D investment.
- Identify possible patent infringers.
- Identify potential licensees for the company's patents.

On a more engineering-focused note, patent searching—and more specifically reading issued patents in the particular technology or art that the engineer has an interest—will help the engineer or product researcher to quickly learn various approaches to the technology that have worked (and failed) for other inventors in the past. From the legal perspective, patent searching is a critical element in the initial review and patentability qualification of a new invention.

Patent Searches and Novelty

That patentable matter must be novel is a basic requirement for granting a U.S. patent. Patent searches are one of the most thorough ways to help prove the novelty of an invention. We know that any prior art will affect, if not destroy, the novelty of an invention; however, the absence of relevant prior art can reinforce the novelty as well. Some time after the initial invention disclosure has been recorded, a patent search may be conducted to verify patentability. If an initial search indicates that your present invention is not patentable (because prior art exists), then the patent search may enlighten the inventor of design-arounds, improvements, or other elements to the product's present design that may ultimately result in a patent.

Patent Searches and Claims

The scope of the claims in an issued patent should be as broad as possible so as to lay claim to the largest area of the technology; however, it is also important to claim neither too broadly, nor too narrowly. A patent search can help determine whether related art or prior art exists that will help define the claim scope.

Your patent counsel will play an important part in the decision-making process, but the counsel of experts within your group should also be considered. We know claims need to have real-time benefits; this usually relates to some sort of economic advantage, whether that is superior performance, an improved process, or another cost-cutting attribute. So experts on your team (i.e., marketing, manufacturing, and engineering) must provide their expert input, validating the go/no-go decision.

More sophisticated patent researchers can search directly on the actual claims language, using various words to describe operative concepts. A patent strategy for some companies is to intentionally *not* use descriptive words that would be obvious to a researcher in their industry. This allows them to hide a patent application or issued patent until they elect to assert their patent on unsuspecting infringers. As an example, a company that manufactured electrical plugs for cables could refer to the invention as a "molded, multiple conductive blade wire transition device." Reviewing claims that describe an invention using obtuse language could find infringers or patenting opportunities.

Patent Searching and Licensing

Companies that are determined to generate revenue from licensing their patents will need to find licensees. Should companies simply wait and hope that other companies will call them out of the blue, asking if they will license a patent? This is not a very proactive method of finding licensees. Companies that use online patent search tools can identify many potential licensees by researching companies that are very active in a particular technology or by identifying companies that may be infringing a patent. Patent owners are fond of saying that infringers make great licensees.

Patent Searches, Analytics, and Trending

An entirely new collection of patent analytics tools is emerging in the marketplace that allow for not only searching, but also analyzing the search results. The result is that the researcher can discover more information related to a competitor's technology, trends in a particular patent field, or analysis of any number of other time, technology, competitor, or language factors.

How does one find the patent data to analyze? Searching patent databases will usually provide an incredible collection of data that can then be moved into an analytical process—either on a desktop computer, or via the Internet. Searchable patent databases are available from most of the major patent authorities, such as the U.S. Patent & Trademark Office, the European Patent Office, and others, as well as from a handful of commercial patent data providers.

Until now, it was not possible to perform a global patent search with a single query (one had to access each patent database individually), but *www.IPSearchEngine.com* has brought together the largest collection of patent data in a single searchable database to help speed the accuracy, relevancy, and breadth of searches for patent data.

Patent analytic tools vary in capability, so it's important to scan through them all to see if and how such analytic power can be applied to your patent strategy.

Companies providing patent analytics tools are *www.wisdomain.com, www.winslab.com,* and *http://ERP.patentcafe.com* by PatentCafé. IPSearch-Engine is Web-based (rather than software installed on a computer), the advantage therein being that patents do not need to be downloaded to conduct the analysis, and the analysis can be run in real time.

Who Conducts the Searches?

Although almost anyone can conduct a patent search, certain levels of legal and technical skill and experience are required for various levels of patent searching. For instance, patentability or infringement searches should be conducted by a professional patent researcher or patent attorney. In contrast, preliminary patent searching by an engineer may be sufficient to determine if a certain new discovery he or she has made can be patented.

IN THE REAL WORLD

Contributory Infringement

Thorough patent searching can quickly verify if a new discovery is infringing previously patented matter or if it would cause the infringement of an existing patent. This search can be particularly important to your company because causing the infringement (sometimes called inducing infringement) of another patent carries the same legal consequences as simple patent infringement itself.

It could also be disastrous for your company to spend time and money on pursuing a technology that is going to cause the ultimate infringement of one or more existing patents. Not only would it be a litigation nightmare, but more important, it would most likely destroy your ability to license out your technology.

Technology or state-of-the-art searches can be conducted by a company's engineers, patent researchers, or patent legal professionals. The intention of the search drives who should be conducting it. If the engineer wants to learn about the state of the art—in fact, learn what core technology their competitor may be pursuing—then the engineer will glean more technical information from a patent search than a patent attorney might. A patent attorney looking for claims language that would suggest possible infringement would certainly have an entirely different objective, and would be looking for legal claims language.

The patent strategy established by the PQM Team will include clear objectives for all departments. Once established and initiated, new inventive discoveries, changes in laws, and market opportunities may cause you to alter that strategy somewhat. Your PQM Team can decide; however, another important factor will come into play that may influence your strategy as well. Just like wise military generals establish their wartime strategies, they also rely heavily on day-to-day tactics to win the many battles. Just like those generals, there are patent tactics you can use as an arsenal of weapons to augment your strategy.

CHAPTER 4

Patent Tactics

 After reading this chapter you will be able to

- Understand patent tactics to create a more effective patent program
- Learn specific techniques to slow down patent issuance— why and how to do it
- Learn specific techniques to speed up patent issuance— why and how to do it
- Learn how to defer patent application costs
- Learn how to keep the invention secret for a longer period
- Learn how to frustrate your competitor's patent strategy
- Understand patent claims tactics

Establishing a patent strategy is important; it sets the long-term objectives that will subsequently drive more narrow decision making related to the intellectual property plan. Now what?

Tactics! Putting the strategy into play, one piece at a time, is the essence of patent tactics. It's not the intention of this chapter to turn every engineer or financial strategist into a patent tactician. Rather, every reader who gets a taste of patent tactics will be a better informed, more effective, and much more valuable PQM Team player. By identifying possible tactics, every member of your team can bring suggestions to the table that the patent attorney may never have been given reason to ask or can identify early tactics that a competitor may be using against your company.

We are not suggesting that you implement any of these tactics. Tactics, as in war, do not always produce the desired result. They should only be implemented by senior business and legal staff who understand the offensive and negative implications of each tactic; however, in the real world of patent maneuvering, competitive positioning, and risk reduction, it's important to keep in mind various tactics and to understand how and why they may be used—both by and against you. Together with your patent attorney, your PQM Team will decide whether any or all of the patent tactics should be brought into the company's arsenal.

Some tactics are intended to rush a patent filing through the patent office more quickly than another patent. Some tactics are intended to delay the patent issuance or hide the patent so a competitor will have difficulty finding it even if it issues. The following list is far from exhaustive, but it does cover some of the more practiced tactics you are likely to run into, such as:

- Slowing down patent issuance
- Speeding up patent issuance
- Deferring patent application costs
- Keeping the invention secret for a longer time
- Frustrating a competitor's patent strategy
- Using patent claims tactics

As U.S. and international patent laws continually change, the ability to use those laws to particular business advantage will continue to change. Corporate and patent counsel will ideally be up on these changes, but legal professionals often overlook the significance of law changes with respect to business tactics. All members of the PQM Team must remain vigilantly aware of law changes and possible new patent tactics and bring new information to the attention of the team. Here is an essential overview of the whys and hows of patent tactics.

Slowing Down Patent Issuance

There are many reasons to delay prosecution or issuance of a patent application. Getting your patent issued quickly is not always the best tactic.

Once a patent is issued, it is published and becomes a public document (patent applications are published at 18 months after filing regardless of whether they have yet issued). At that time, competitors will know what was patented and can attempt to design around the invention if they believe they can. Delaying patent issuance may help keep the invention or the underlying inventive matter secret for a longer period. The longer a patent remains unpublished, the higher the likelihood is that somebody will infringe your patent when it issues. Also, the likelihood that an infringing company will become a reluctant licensee increases with the company's investment in the infringing product.

If a new product is sold into the marketplace and is marked with a Patent-Pending notice, however, it may be a strong deterrent for others to not infringe the anticipated patented matter. Doing so could be extremely costly to the infringing party because once the patent issues, it could be forced to either license the technology or cease and desist sales and production. Such a case could be disastrous and is an abuse of shareholder trust. Worse, with knowledge of an issued patent, the infringing party would be vulnerable to willful infringement and liable for treble damages.

Delaying patent issuance may include extending the prosecuting time frame to file one or more continuation-in-part (CIP) applications to try to improve the scope of the patent protection, preserve cash flow by spreading attorney fees over a longer period, or extend the patent-

Big Budget Impact

Under the 21st Century Strategic Plan, applications for CIPs or divisional applications will be heavily penalized. A patent filed with patently indistinct claims when compared to another application you have filed will require a surcharge of $10,000 per each previously filed patent. Therefore, a careful assessment of the trade-offs between much higher fees and multiple patents to extend or delay patent issuance need to be weighed by patent counsel, the CFO, and the PQM Team.

pending time frame if abandonment of the application is eminent or the scope of protection is going to be easy to design around.

Divisional Applications

One tactic commonly used is to file a single patent application that contains several related inventive matters. The benefits to doing this are as follows:

- Defers patent filing fees
- Allows filing many patents over time, but with same priority date
- Delays issuance on the patentable matter

When filing a patent application, regardless of how much inventive matter it contains, you will pay a single application fee. When the examiner makes his or her first review of the application, you will receive an office action rejecting the application based on it containing "more than one invention" or "unrelated inventive matter." The examiner will cite the various "inventive matters," and you can then make decisions about the order in which they should be prosecuted.

This action is referred to as a divisional patent application in which the contents are split out into two or more patent applications. When you file applications with multiple inventions, the inventive matter is reviewed sequentially by the patent examiner in the order you select. This extends the application review time frame. If there are three or four different matters to consider, it may take a few years to complete the examination process. This does not mean that the life of the patent when issued is extended because the subsequent reviews are limited to the term of the initial filing date; however, it does delay issuance and preserve cash outlay.

There are two common approaches to creating divisional patent applications. One is to include inventive matter that will claim (1) the product, (2) the process in which it is made, and (3) a method of use. This would usually be split out into two or three separate applications depending on the relationship between the three inventive matters. Those matters that are specific only to the present invention may be kept together in one application. Any inventive matters that have a broader scope and may apply to other applications outside of the present invention will be split out.

A second approach is simply to include several inventive elements regarding the invention. For instance, a new plastic bag may include (1) directional-tear perforations, (2) a stronger handle, (3) a self-opening method of use, and (4) ventilation to allow condensation to escape. All of these matters may be separately patentable and would be split out. This example could even be further compounded by illustrating different uses for the directional perforations and various bag styles for the self-opening method.

The form that is used to continue to the prosecution of a divisional application is called a Continued Prosecution Application (CPA) Request Transmittal.

Missing Parts

This topic refers to filing permanent patent applications. Although filing an application with missing parts may be a helpful tactic to save time and meet a priority date, it typically results in other delays instead, such as:

- Delaying payment of filing fee
- Delaying delivery of information not yet ready to file
- Delaying 18-month publication

Filing the permanent application with or without certain pertinent parts of the application can also extend the review period. Typically, missing parts could include any one or more components such as the Inventor's Declaration, or Oath of Inventorship, drawings, or in the case of a plant patent, photographs.

For instance, filing an application to meet a certain crucial date, such as the expiration date of a provisional patent application, may be done without the inventor's signature, if the inventor is not available to sign the original documents. The patent office will respond with a Notice of Missing Parts, which are then submitted at this later date. This may delay the review period up to 90 days.

Time Extensions

A common tactic employed during the patent-pending and examination phase is to ask for an extension on your response to office action. When an office action is received, you have 90 days to respond. You may ask for an extension on this time period for a fee. This is accomplished by submitting a form entitled Petition for Extension of Time Under 37 CFR 1.136 (a). You may request up to five months' extension; however, this can cost $2,000 or more.

Delay Issuance

Once the claims in an application have been approved, a notice of allowance is received by the inventor. From receipt of this notice, the inventor, or owner (assignee), then pays the issue fee to the Patent and Trademark Office (PTO). You may take up to 90 days to submit this final payment, thus delaying issuance. Upon receipt, it normally takes about three months for the patent to issue, but at times it can take longer, up to six months. During this time period it may be desirable to file a CIP application on related inventive matter.

Continuation-in-Part Applications

During innovation development in which one or more patents are pending, new, related inventive matter may be discovered that would broaden patent protection. If this inventive matter is either newly discovered or perhaps something that is now understood in a different manner, it most likely would not have been included in the original patent applications. Thus patent protection of the new subject matter can be pursued, and the original priority filing date preserved, by filing a CIP application describing the new matter.

It may sound a bit unbelievable, but when developing new concepts, it is not always easy to understand the true inventive matter. We tend to think in terms of simple, physical inventions and not as much in terms of how they may be used in a system or in combination with other components. Filing CIP applications to cover the new inventive matter is a common administrative action.

The alternate to filing a CIP on new inventive matter is to file a new patent application, either provisional or nonprovisional. The benefit of filing a new application is that a new priority date is established on the new inventive matter, thus lengthening the patent protection of the technology. One of the factors influencing your choice to file a new application or a CIP is whether a public disclosure has been made. If a public disclosure has been made, a CIP may be essential to protect your right to file an application and avoid the one-year rule. If not, you will have to consider if there is any vulnerability to having the later priority date if a new application is filed. Delaying issuance is accomplished by the Continued Prosecution Application (CPA) Request Transmittal.

Refiling PPAs

When new products have been conceived, PPAs are filed while development is being delayed, stalled, or is simply taking longer than originally anticipated. An uncommon tactic that many may consider dangerous is to refile an existing PPA. Providing the inventive matter has not been publicly disclosed during this initial development, your rights may not have been sacrificed. There are two sides to this argument.

First, when refiling a PPA, the priority filing date on the first PPA is lost; however, refiling a PPA may also contribute to the paper trail, thus reinforcing first-to-invent rights. Refiling a PPA is a tactic that should only be used in an emergency to either preserve cash flow or perhaps prevent an errant public disclosure without patent protection, if it is impossible to file the permanent application in time.

Reissue Applications

Within two years from the grant of the original patent, a patentee may file a reissue application and attempt to enlarge the scope of the original claims to include the disclosed but previously unclaimed subject matter. Claims may not be broadened thereafter. In such a case, a reexamination is your request to either add language that clarifies the breadth of the scope or add new claims. The new claims must be directly related to the inventive matter discussed in the application.

If the examiner agrees to the new claims or the new clarifications, the result is the granting of a reissue patent. The term of the new patent will be limited to the 20-year period beginning with the filing date of the original patent application.

Patent Appeals Court

At times, an examiner will not be convinced that the scope in your application's claims is valid, possibly because of a difference of opinion between the parties, an insufficient understanding of the involved technology, or even a difference of opinion in the interpretation of patent laws. For instance, you may disagree with what an examiner cites as relevant. In such an impasse, a final rejection may result, thus requiring you to have the application reviewed by the Board of Patent Appeals. With your request, the examiner will send a Notice of Appeal to the board.

Patent applications reviewed by the board run about 33 percent in favor of the inventor's argument and about 67 percent in favor of the examiner's. These are not hopeless odds, and your legal counsel should have sufficient experience in these matters to understand the nature of the examiner's final rejection and to determine your chances of winning an appeal. For instance, if the final rejection is based on an examiner's misplaced reference of equivalence of use, the chances are probably high that the rejection would be overturned.

Speeding Up Patent Issuance

It normally takes about six to nine months to receive your first office action after submitting a patent application. It is sometimes advantageous to accelerate the review of a patent application in order to expedite issuance. This may be particularly valuable if a competitor begins using your technology or if you are anticipating the infringement of the technology you are developing. With technologies that are short lived, such as many software applications, you can use this tactic to protect and lengthen the short life span of your technology.

It may also be a valuable tool if you have a potential license agreement pending, based on the outcome of the review of the patent application. There are two broad courses you can take: one is based on taking the appropriate administrative action, and the other is a Petition to Make Special.

Administrative Action

There are several common-sense things you can do to get a patent to issue sooner:

- *File promptly.* Once you understand the inventive matter, file a permanent patent application right away.

- *Limit the patent application to inventive matter that will not be split out into a divisional application.* As has already been mentioned, this adds time and complexity to the filing process.

- *Do the patent search for the examiner.* Include copies of all relevant patents. Better yet, have the search documents delivered in person shortly after the arrival of the patent application itself so they don't get lost in the application's documents.

- *Respond promptly to office actions.* Most inventors and legal counsel tend to wait toward the end of the allotted response period of 90 days. Responding promptly when office actions are received can save months.

The sum total of such an approach can literally subtract several months from the patent pending period. Make sure all your responses are sent via verifiable means, such as Express Mail, UPS, or Federal Express; or if possible, deliver them in person.

Petition to Make Special 2.8

If an inventor is about to die or an invention is an important breakthrough that has major implications toward a national concern, a company may file a Petition to Make Special. If the petition is approved, the application will move ahead of all others and the examination process is expedited.

Inventions that are afforded priority include those that meet the following criteria:

- Prevent terrorism
- Materially improve or enhance the environment

- Contribute to the development or conservation of energy
- Are related to cures for AIDS and cancer

The purpose of this rule is to help get these inventions into the hands of those who need them more quickly. There is no additional cost associated with these types of priority petitions.

A petition to make an application special may also be submitted on grounds other than those previously cited for a nominal fee (set forth in § 1.17(h)). These exceptions are granted under the following conditions:

- A prospective manufacturer has sufficient capital and the facilities to manufacture the invention in quantity or sufficient capital and facilities will be made available if a patent is granted.
- A prospective manufacturer will not manufacture, or will not increase present manufacture, unless a certain patent will be granted.

TIPS & TECHNIQUES

A potential licensee may occasionally be reluctant to enter into a license agreement in fear that a pertinent patent may not issue with sufficiently broad coverage to protect the technology. This may be an excellent reason to submit a Petition to Make Special. If you then encounter difficulty convincing the patent examiner to issue the patent with sufficient scope, this is an excellent reason to make a personal visit to the patent office with your legal counsel to discuss the worthiness. In fact, if you have a potential licensee that is ready to take on the technology, that fact in itself may be sufficient to verify the value and merit of the inventive matter.

- A prospective manufacturer obligates itself to manufacture the invention, in the United States or its possessions, in quantity immediately upon the allowance of claims or issuance of a patent, which will protect the investment.

When submitting the petition, the applicant or assignee includes a statement purporting a careful and thorough search of the prior art or has a good knowledge of the pertinent prior art. The applicant must also provide copies of the references deemed most closely related to the subject matter encompassed by the claims. A Petition to Make Special (708.02) is provided for under 37 Code of Federal Regulations (C.F.R.), Section 1.102 Advancement of Examination.

Accelerating 18-Month Publication

Now that we've seen why some people use the delay in publication of a patent application to their tactical advantage, why would one want to publish early?

A patent application is prior art as of its filing date. This means that if a patent application is published earlier rather than later, it will service as prior art that would effectively eliminate a competitor's ability to file a patent on the published, disclosed invention.

One patent strategy discussed in a previous chapter was "Patent the tree—cut the forest." In other words, file the patent on the best embodiment of the innovation in question, and disclose all other possibilities and spin-offs from that core patent so others cannot patent them. Because of the low cost of filing a PPA, companies that file many—even 50 or 60—PPAs on variations or different embodiments of a single invention can later decide which one(s) they want to file a nonprovisional application on. The rest of the PPAs that the company elects to not pursue can be published early, thereby becoming prior art that prevents others from patenting around the core technology.

Four Tracks Equals Reduced Pendency

Under the 21st Century Strategic Plan, which proposed to break down the patent filing process into four tracks, patent applications may be *accelerated* through the process by (1) expediting the outside contracted prior art search report, and (2) paying the application and examination fee at the same time. Under the new plan, the target pendency is only 18 months *after request for examination and payment of examination fees.*

On the other hand, one can *delay* the patent issuance considerably under the new plan by (1) filing a PPA, (2) filing a nonprovisional application 12 months later, (3) requesting examination 18 months after the filing date (currently proposed period at the time of this writing), and (4) filing the examination request with missing parts, and slowly responding to objections. The pendency, provided every avenue was exercised, could approach four years.

Elements of the proposed PTO Strategic Plan are sure to change with little notice, so it's imperative that your PQM Team stay abreast of the most current changes.

Deferring Patent Application Costs

Of all the previously discussed methods to either speed up or delay the patent examination and issue process, many of them also defer the cost of patenting. This is accomplished by either deferring the associated fees or postponing attorney actions, thus deferring legal fees. Those most notable methods include the following:

- Applying the one-year rule
- Filing divisional applications

- Filing with missing parts
- Submitting extended time extensions
- Filing CIPs
- Filing and refiling PPAs

Keeping the Invention Secret for a Longer Period

The 18-month patent pregrant publication ensures that *most* U.S. patent applications filed after November 2001 will be published 18 months after filing (causing the secret aspects of the patent application to become public).

A nonpublication request must be submitted concurrently with the filed application. Therefore, applicants who prefer nonpublication and have not previously filed a foreign (or international) application that is subject to 18-month publication should consider filing nonpublication requests at the time of filing, even if they have not yet decided whether to file outside the United States. If the applicant subsequently decides to file a foreign (or international) application that will publish after 18 months, however, he or she must notify the USPTO within 45 days after the date of such filing.

Delaying 18-Month Patent Pregrant Publication

Filing a notice of intent to not file a foreign patent eliminates the requirement that a U.S. application be published. This procedure to avoid publication, which informs others of your invention before your patent issues, is intended to be used only for U.S. patents. You must request nonpublication at the time of filing, along with certification that the application will not be filed in foreign markets. (There are some important notifications to the Patent Office that your patent attorney must stay on top of to prevent abandonment.)

To publish or not to publish? Under the American Inventor Protection Act (AIPA), patent applications filed on and after May 29, 2000 will generally be published 18 months after filing. This is already a requirement with European and most developed countries; the United States is joining the process only recently. An application also becomes a prior art document as of its filing date.

There are several reasons to not have a patent application made public—one being that the inventor or ultimate patent owner wishes to keep the invention secret for a while longer. This ploy can frequently be used to keep the patent information away from competitors, so that they make the investment in the market or product with a technology that will infringe your patent. In other words, it allows the competition to become positioned so that licensing could become their least costly option to remain in the business.

Frustrating a Competitor's Patent Strategy
Third-Party Prior Art Submissions

Although not specifically authorized by Subtitle E of the AIPA, the USPTO has added 37 CFR section 1.99 to permit third-party submissions of patents and publications that are relevant to pending published applications, subject to the following:

- Patents and publications submitted under this section will be entered into the application file, but not necessarily considered or cited by the examiner.

- Submissions under this section must be served on the applicant.

- Submissions under this section must be filed within two months from the date the application publishes or before the mailing date of a Notice of Allowance, whichever is earlier.

- Submissions under this section must not include an explanation of the patents or publications provided therewith.

The USPTO apparently believes that permitting third-party prior art submissions will improve the quality of examination and issued patents by making more relevant prior art available to the examiner. It appears likely, however, that the inability to explain the relevance of submitted prior art will dissuade third-party submissions. Generally, third parties will not be sufficiently confident that the examiner will independently recognize the significance of, or properly apply, submitted prior art. If the examiner cites but does not maintain a rejection based on the submitted prior art, a strong presumption of validity over the submitted prior art will arise. Most likely, third parties will prefer saving highly relevant prior art for reexamination or litigation proceedings, during which they can advocate a position that the prior art either raises a substantial new question of patentability, establishes invalidity, or both.

New Category of Prior Art for Published Applications

Section 4505 of the AIPA amends 35 USC section 102(e) to create a new category of prior art. Specifically, patentability is precluded when the claimed invention is described in "[a printed patent] application . . . by another filed in the United States before the invention by the application for patent." This new category of prior art, which will make published U.S. patent applications an important source of prior art under section 102(e), also extends to published PCT applications filed on or after November 29, 2000 that designate the United States and are published in English.

Reexamination Request

Patent reexamination is used as an affirmative defense to infringement claims, but it is also used to undermine the validity of a targeted competitor's patent. Effectively, the party calling for the reexamination may present the PTO with prior art that may invalidate the competitor's prior issued patent; however, once the party asks the PTO for a reexamination of an issued patent, the patent holder gets to comment to the private ruling, and then that prior art can no longer be used in any court cases.

In other words, if you ask for a reexamination of a competitor's patent based on prior art you believe is your silver bullet, you get one chance to present your evidence to the PTO. If the PTO upholds the validity, you may still file suit if you believe it's warranted, but you will not be able to use that prior art later in litigation during a jury trial.

Interference

Interference is an action that may be initiated by the PTO to determine who is the first true inventor of a particular subject matter. The inter-

PROPOSED 2003 PATENT OFFICE RULES

Third Parties Can Frustrate Your Patent Process

Under the 21st Century Strategic Plan four-track patent process, third parties may challenge an issued patent any time during the first 12 months following issuance. The precise process for filing such a challenge with the U.S. Patent Office was not published at the time of this writing; however, the challenge will be decided by an administrative judge at the U.S. PTO rather than in the court system. This means that under the proposed new 2003 rules, a third-party challenge, and hence frustration to a competitor, will be less expensive than an interference and much easier than a reexamination request. As always, understand that the actual rules may differ from the proposed rules, so ask your patent counsel for the current published PTO policy and review how you can use those new rules to your tactical advantage.

ference proceeding may be initiated between two pending applications or between an application and an already granted patent, providing the granted patent was not issued more than one year before filing the new application.

Although this is not a simple administrative action that frustrates a competitor, it is certainly an action that can be taken when you have been made aware of a competitor's application on an inventive matter that you have been developing and are confident of your priority position. Notifying the PTO would instigate the proceeding.

Fewer than 1 out of 1,500 applications received by the U.S. Patent Office will be involved in an interference proceeding. According to Ian Calvert, an administrative patent judge at the USPTO, about 52.5 percent of the proceedings were in favor of the senior party, 31.7 percent in favor of the junior party, 9.4 percent resulted in no patents being issued, 5.8 percent involved no interference, and 0.7 percent resulted in a split award.

In such a proceeding, both parties submit facts supporting two factors. The first is the date of original conception, which refers to the first, original date the inventor conceived the inventive matter. The second is the date of reduction to practice, which refers to the date on which the invention was proven to work the way that the inventor says it works. This is usually proven by the construction of a prototype or by drawings. If there are no functional drawings or prototypes, the filing date of a regular application completely disclosing the invention is treated as the equivalent of the date of reduction of practice. If there are also no log books or other supporting facts and materials, then the filing date of the application would be considered the earliest date of both the date of original conception and reduction to practice. Thus the importance of maintaining detailed log books, records, and archives is clear.

After all is said and done, the best way to frustrate your competitors' efforts is to out-think and out-invent them. Try to anticipate future

Patent Office Facts

Information from the Patent Office reveals that interference annually affects about 35 to 40 patents filed by small companies and independent inventors. Of these, only about eight more inventors in the senior position will retain the first-to-invent status over those in the junior position, which is about what one would expect. Because interference occurs in less than 1 of every 1,500 patents filed, it is not worth any worry.

needs and customer wants. Don't be afraid to attack yourself, and always try to invent the next generation product or system before your competitor does.

Patent Claims Tactics

Several factors and administrative actions can affect the scope of a patent's claims. You and your counsel can discuss them. Sometimes claims can be expanded upon or broadened with the use of CIPs, requests to reissue, and by submitting to the Patent Appeals court.

Scope of Claims Language

Corporate inventors and engineers should already be keeping inventor's journals. When making entries, they should broaden patent claim language whenever they are documenting the invention. When corporate patent counsel receives the description from the inventor, they will understand the importance of broadening the claims language at certain critical points.

Use the phrase "fastening means" versus "screw" or "glue." Use "plurality" rather than "two" or "three," which restricts your claims to two or three, but not four. This language can be broadened.

Doctrine of Equivalents

The Doctrine of Equivalents was established in 1950 and has been the subject of many court cases over the years. Simply stated, it says:

If the elements of a product do not literally infringe a patent's claims, but essentially serve the same function, then a claim of infringement is still valid.

This definition is now commonly used and was determined by the U.S. Supreme Court in a case commonly referred to as the Hilton-Davis case. More recently, the Festo case just decided by the U.S. Supreme Court determined that claims should be interpreted more literally, turning the clock back on the earlier Hilton-Davis case.

The best way to use the Doctrine of Equivalents in your strategy is simply to try *not* to rely on it. If the breadth of scope of a claim can best be described by simple, broad language, that's what you want. Frankly, this is what your patent attorneys get paid for anyway—protecting your assets with patents that have bulletproof claims.

Relying on the literal interpretation of a claim in a competitor's patent can be dangerous. To better protect the company's interests (and those of its shareholders), and to avoid the potential of an expensive lawsuit, a broader interpretation of their meanings is probably wise. After all, that's how you would expect others to interpret your claims. Regardless of how claims are interpreted, your legal counsel should have the final word.

In Festo's case, the court determined that a claim that had to be modified during prosecution must be interpreted literally instead of figuratively according to the Doctrine of Equivalents. In light of this ruling, one practice used today when prosecuting patent applications is to not modify any submitted claims, but simply add on new ones, or to include a multitude of claims written in various language so that at least a few of them are accepted. Which of these administrative tactics is the most appropriate is a decision best determined by your PQM Team leader and your patent attorney.

Keep in mind that some patent claims might have to be interpreted more literally than other claims anyway. This is usually the case when claims have specific attributes that had to be included for the examiner to award the patent.

PROPOSED 2003 PATENT OFFICE RULES

Post-Festo Tactic Could Increase Costs

Following the initial Festo ruling, a new tactic emerged that promised the ability to avoid the loss of claims that were amended while a patent was pending. That tactic was filing many small claims, possibly into the thousands for a single patent application. With so many precise and marginally distinct claims, a patentee would simply need to delete a claim if the examiner objected, but there would be little likelihood that one of the claims would need to be amended (and if no amendments, no problems under the *Festo* ruling).

The 21st Century Strategic Plan, in part intended to "change the behavior of patentees," heavily penalizes the patentee for making more than five independent claims or more than 20 total claims in a patent application. Now, instead of recklessly writing hundreds of claims, the financial benefit to the decision will need to be weighed.

Review the new patent application fees and the finally approved language regarding filing excessive claims and decide with your PQM Team the best policy regarding filing patents with many claims.

If the breadth of claims is important to your patent, which is true in most cases, remember that when you are inventing the next generation, your claims tend to be much broader as well. When developing new concepts and products, it is always a good idea to keep that future-thinking concept in mind.

CHAPTER 5

Managing Patents in the Marketing Department

After reading this chapter you will be able to

- Understand marketing's IP and product development focus

- Understand the difference between methods of use or systems patents, improvement patents, design patents, trade dress, and copyrights

- Learn the critical elements that will offer your company the competitive marketing edge

- Learn how to establish a patent plan in marketing

Patents mean more to the marketing department than to almost all the others. Being a legal monopoly means legally being able to sell products that competitors can't. To the marketing department, patents can represent superior products, greater sales, higher profits, a more secure market position, and longer product life cycles.

Although marketers tend to focus on sales and building the brand name, there is simply no better way to protect the name than by patents. This is especially true in the early stages of new product launches. Initially patents can protect a new product launch against knockoffs. With 20 years of patent protection, trademark recognition is built into and embedded in the minds of consumers. Over the long term, the trademark becomes of much greater value, but it could not have been established without the initial patent protection. Some excellent examples are General Electric's lightbulb (GE), Hoover's vacuum, Xerox's copiers, and Dow's Zip-Loc bags. Patents allowed these companies to ramp up and establish major product lines and trademarks.

The primary objectives of patents in the marketing department are to identify those opportunities that can increase sales and profitability of existing products, extend a product's life cycle, and develop new concepts into new products for product line expansion, whether those patents or technology are developed internally or licensed in.

To do this, the focus is generally product-based protection, which covers several types of patent protection, but the marketing department should have a keen awareness of the various forms of patent protection and intellectual property that can affect the company's future profitability.

 TIPS & TECHNIQUES

Increasingly, software search tools that access patent databases are being used by the engineering and legal deaprtments; however, marketing departments can now benefit from this data mining capability. By using this same patent database as an information core, marketing managers can model a competitor's patent or R&D activity and can visualize the technology trends being pursued— an early warning device that can alert marketing managers to a competitor's attitude toward new product development.

Patent data can also indicate which areas of product development a competitor is pursuing, and in contrast, those they are *not* pursuing, pointing toward markets and niches your competitors most likely will not enter. While the legal department is more interested in patent prior art, the marketing department would have little interest in reading patent claims.

Emerging data analysis and mining tools available online include *http://ERP.patentcafe.com, www.IPSearchEngine.com, www.wisdo main.com,* and *www.winslab.com.*

Marketing's IP and Product Development Focus

For the most part, all patents developed within the corporation affect the marketing department because they will ultimately reflect on profitablity directly or indirectly. Patents covering a newly developed innovation or a simple improvement will have a direct impact, whereas a patented production process or an item of safety within the manufacturing department will have an indirect impact on marketing and profit potential.

The focus in this chapter is on those patents that have a direct impact on the marketing department and how the marketing department can solicit and identify viable, profitable opportunities. This is the central focus of the PQM system in the marketing department, with a secondary responsibility to confirm and verify other innovations outside the marketing department that may have an impact on product performance or functionality.

In this light, marketing has a responsibility to stay abreast of competitive developments in the field and to act in an R&D capacity to the engineering department to field competitive information and identify emerging customer needs and desires. This point gets right at the heart of developing new trends—those that represent long-term profit potential. In summary, your department's central focus will include the following form of patent protection and IP opportunities.

Product Patents

All new product releases should include product patent protection if at all possible. Some companies will not even consider going into a marketplace without patent protection. Marketing's product group focus should also include developing and patenting any new elements or devices that may be incorporated into their existing product line. These may either be developed internally or licensed in.

Methods of Use or Systems Patents

One of the most important tasks of any marketing department is to identify new opportunities, which often come about by identifying existing problems. Those problems that the marketing department identifies that have to do with ease of use may be solvable by the use of a new, unique system. Systems save time, reduce steps, and decrease errors. If your marketing team can identify some of these opportunities, they can bring them to the PQM Team for evaluation.

For instance, if your company developed laser technology for scanning bar codes, what would be some other applications and uses besides scanning retail products? The technology can also be used on cartons for inventory control, in-store coupons, even a method of identifying patients and patient needs in hospitals. The opportunities are endless, and these kinds of new applications are usually discovered by the marketing department. Is your department providing this type of feedback to engineering?

Keep in mind that systems patents tend to make products people friendly. One example is how PCs did not become mass-marketed products until Apple made them easy to use, and frankly, easy to sell as well. Is your marketing department aware of the difficulties of using your products? Are they sensitive to the way customers use your products? When the product is used, what errors are the customers experiencing? How can these problems be corrected?

Systems patents may provide greater opportunity for marketing than any other patent group. For instance, the first patent on the common style of plastic grocery sack with the strap handles resulted in some sales, but when Sonoco Products Company elevated the use of the sack into a self-opening system used on a dispensing rack, it dramatically increased the sack's usage and sales. If plastic grocery sacks were hard to use, they would not have been used, but once the Sonoco system was introduced in the late 1980s, its plastic grocery sack sales soared and rapidly began to replace paper as the preferred bag.

Systems patents represent a great opportunity for companies. The marketing department can identify these opportunities by staying close to the customer. It might be difficult for customers to articulate their needs, but smart, perceptive marketing people can meet the challenge.

Improvement Patents

Marketing's responsibilities also include identifying improvements that may be protected by improvement patents. Some product patents and systems patents may also be called improvement patents. For instance, the previously described plastic grocery sack system was an improvement over the prior art grocery sack, but so may a simple, innovative element of an existing product be called an improvement patent. It really does not matter how you categorize what an improvement is, what's important is to take action when opportunities arise that allow you to improve an existing product's performance—no matter how small it may seem.

It's important to understand that improvements to existing products or systems that qualify as novel, unique, and useful inventive matter may be patented by anyone, regardless of who owns an underlying patent or who is manufacturing the present product. So why not have your department initiate the patent and product development instead?

Design Patents

We know that design patents refer only to ornamental design and not functional design and do not usually afford much patent protection, but there can be exceptions. For instance, Nike has used design patents in its shoe designs with substantial success. Their primary purpose is to keep others from cloning their attractive shoe designs and shapes. Thus design patents can help preserve an original, proprietary look and have a positive effect on marketability. Design patents may also accompany products that are protected under separate utility patents for their functional utility.

Utility patents are generally considered the better patent protection, but there are applications when a simple design patent may serve the desired purpose. Generally speaking, the wiser choice is to strive to secure utility patent protection whenever possible. It is wise to seek design patent protection only if the ornamental design will have some important, lasting proprietary effect on marketability that is not easy for others to design around.

Trade Dress

Trade dress is a type of trademark or copyright that applies primarily to product and package designs and configurations. Your package designs can be protected against unfair competition if they meet three basic criteria: (1) nonfunctionality, (2) proof of secondary meaning, or (3) likelihood of confusion. The common law tort of unfair competition has given protection against copying nonfunctional aspects of consumer products.

Some examples cited in common law actions include the configuration of a cereal biscuit, a loaf of bread, a medicinal tablet, a root beer bottle, a cologne bottle, a crescent wrench, a washing machine, a clock, and a padlock.

The marketing department should consider registering trade dress along with any new products that will be protected by patents. Unlike patents, which expire in 20 years, or a design patent, which expires in only 14 years, trade dress may be renewed indefinitely. Although it may be arguably similar in definition to a design patent, trade dress can have a long-term impact. After years of use it becomes an intellectual property that is more valuable than the patent. Your legal department can determine if trade dress protection or design patent protection is best to pursue. You can learn about trade dress in depth in *Essentials of Intellectual Property.*

Copyrights

Along with patent applications, copyrights should also be filed when they pertain to the patented matter or the new product being developed. Copyrights protect the writings of an author, artist, or designer. They protect the form of expression, not the subject matter or content. Names and titles do not fall under copyright laws. Copyrights that may enhance the marketing department's patenting efforts are as follows:

- Art used on packaging
- Written copy used on packaging
- Manuals and training-related CDs, videos, and so on
- Software
- Artwork, patterns, and designs

A copyright arises the moment the work is completed. When a work is published, or used in commerce, marking it with a copyright notice gives notice of ownership. A notice essentially warns others of ownership and that damages can be granted if others copy the mark and use it for personal profit or if the commercial value of the copyright is harmed, regardless of profit gained by use of the copyrighted material. Materials copyrighted after January 1, 1978 last the lifetime of the author plus 70 years. For proper marking of your company's copyrights, consult with your legal counsel.

Free ads promoting copyrighted materials are not considered fair use. It is up to the owner to determine if it is okay. Also, it is interesting to note that government publications and notices are not protected by copyright laws. They can be freely copied and disseminated by anyone.

Copyrights are registered with the Copyright Office of the Library of Congress in Washington, D.C. You can learn more about copyrights in *Essentials of Intellectual Property.*

The Competitive Marketing Edge

Nothing may affect sales and profit potential or the life of the corporation more than patents, regardless of whether they are developed internally, licensed in, or cross-licensed. The PQM system qualifies which patents will give you the most advantageous marketing edge.

A Legal Monopoly

Patents give the owner a sovereign granted monopoly in exchange for disclosing the inventive technology to the public for the benefit of society as a whole. Patent protection is like building a fence around your product line. It's a legal monopoly that keeps generic competition from copying your products and features.

An initial patent on the first product release starts the 20-year monopoly. More important, subsequent patents on new improvements and breakthroughs can extend the monopoly because they will endure for 20 years after their filing.

New Product Launches

There is no better way to protect new product launches than by patents. Whether the new product is a new lightbulb, facial tissue, or sandwich bag, patent protection allows the corporation to aggressively create and establish a market presence and recapture their investment from profits. First-to-market opportunities are no guarantee of market dominance, but history tells us that the first to market has the best opportunity to dominate. Over time, the brand name is established and becomes the industry standard.

Patents Protect the Product's Central and Secondary Themes

Many a corporation's existence is based on a central theme, a central focus in the product line. This central theme appeals to your customers, making them want to buy your products and probably why the innovation was created in the first place. Some excellent examples are that Volvo automobiles focus on safety, Polaroid cameras develop photographs in one minute, and Healthy Choice focuses on natural and low-fat ingredients. What is the central theme of your company's product line? A central theme is key to the product's market positioning, and there is no better way to protect that positioning than by patents.

Almost all product lines also have secondary themes, supported by other positioning statements to address them. Secondary themes are usually made after the initial development has progressed and at times after a product has been launched. They could be a result of customer responses, trials, or new needs of the various buying influences such as retailers, distributors, operations managers, and even accountants and warehouse people. Patents are also an excellent way to protect these marketing advantages.

A primary objective of the PQM system in the marketing department is to protect the unique marketing position as well as the secondary marketing positions of the product line. Without some form of protection, competitors can adapt to new market trends and, at times, completely destroy a newly introduced marketing position.

Product Life Extension

Established product lines rarely stay static forever. New improvements must be developed in order to continue market prowess and to adapt to changes in attitudes and customer buying trends. A marketing department that is fast, flexible, and focused can adapt to these new trends—in fact, anticipate them—and protect products with patents.

Although patents may protect the initial market launch, it is commonly known that some time afterward a new breakthrough discovery will be made. A subsequent breakthrough is what really propels sales upward. This is every marketer's dream to discover these breakthrough opportunities, and nothing could be wiser than protecting them by patents. Thus it is usually one of these subsequent improvement patents that gives the significant value for future sales of the product line. These patents not only improve sales revenue but also extend the product's life because there will be an additional 20 years of patent protection from the date of their filings.

Licensed in Expands Product Line

One of the fastest, easiest, and most cost-effective ways to expand sales in a product line is through licensing in. Miller Brewing is a prime example. Miller High Life and Miller Lite beers sold well. Then the company licensed in the cold-filtered brewing process from Sopporo of Japan and

PROPOSED 2003 PATENT OFFICE RULES

Marketers interested in licensing in (to grow a product line, expand market share, and so forth) must be aware that since October 2002, under the proposed 21st Century Strategic Plan, or a version thereof, patent issuance could take four to five years from filing (patent-pending period). Therefore, marketers who are willing to bet on the horse before it races (rather than waiting for a patent to issue before pursuing a licensing agreement) stand to win. Concern about an unfair market advantage competitors might have in the event that a licensed patent does not issue later on can be overcome with a clause in the license agreement voiding the agreement in such a case.

created Miller Genuine Draft. Today, this beer is far and away the best seller of the group.

Opportunities brought to the marketing department by outside entities should be evaluated. Frequently, licensed in opportunities have already been qualified by their inventors regarding market potential and manufacturability. Other times more development may be required. In either case, there are substantial opportunities for the corporation with the right frame of mind and a PQM system to evaluate and manage these opportunities.

Cross-Licensed

One of the best ways to ensure future sales revenues and to standardize product lines is through cross-licensing with friendly competitors. At times, cross-licensing may just keep you in business.

Cross-licensing patents to standardize a product line that is maturing can make it the industry standard and make it difficult for other competing technologies to be introduced. It also extends and establishes your company's technology as the industry standard in the later stages of a product's life cycle.

Cross-licensing may also reduce or eliminate licensing fees and royalties when applying a competitor's patents. At times, cross-licensing may be in your favor and result in a revenue source as well. Of course, all this depends on the values of the cross-licensed patents and their importance toward the security of future sales for the two companies.

One thing is certain: If a company does not have a patent portfolio, it is not in a good negotiating position for cross-licensing, but with bulletproof, relevant patents in the portfolio, there is strength in the negotiating position.

License Out

The marketing department's primary responsibility is sales. When those sales are protected by patents, an envious position may unfold. Establishing a patented product line in the marketplace opens opportunities to license the technology to others.

The benefits are threefold: (1) there is revenue to the corporation and profits for shareholders; (2) it improves the ability to standardize the product line and extends the product cycle; and (3) it tends to point future development efforts in the direction of the patented technology.

An aggressive PQM system in the marketing department that generates patents protecting a product line can be a valuable tool now and in the future.

Ramping up an Industry

In the initial stages of market creation and market development of patented products, there are generally two strategic approaches to ensure maximum market exposure. One approach is to keep the patented matter tightly held and use the technology exclusively for the sole benefit of the corporation and the product line. A second approach is to license out the technology to others in order to ensure that the patented technology quickly becomes the industry standard.

Two important questions to consider when keeping patented matter exclusive are as follows:

1. Will it negatively affect industry conversion and reduce the patented technology to a minor role?

2. If the patented technology is for a substantially new product, such as Velcro, Kleenex, or Xerox plain paper copiers, do you have the resources and wherewithal to ramp up the volume as a sole supplier?

Obviously there are several good examples of companies that have had sufficient resources and market influence to create and develop new markets entirely from within, but there are some bad examples as well. For instance, with the introduction of the VCR, Sony introduced the higher-quality Beta version but wouldn't license it to any others. The rest of the industry could readily license VHS, and thus it become the industry standard. Another example was Apple's unwillingness to standardize its operating and software programs and mouse/icon technologies. How Bill Gates took advantage of that situation is history!

Some product lines are going to need multiple suppliers and competition or they will never be successfully exploited. In many industries, primarily those that are high volume and commodity oriented, multi-

Protect Products During Extended Marketing Period

If the delayed examination period is adopted in one of the forms or modifications of the 21st Century Strategic Plan (as it is expected to be), marketing departments can take advantage of an interesting new strategy of low-cost test marketing.

First, the company may file a PPA followed one year later by the permanent patent application. The permanent patent application will not be examined until the examination fee is paid up to 18 months later. This is a total of 2.5 years in a patent-pending status at controlled expense. During this time frame, test marketing may be conducted and modifications made to improve sales. If the test marketing is not going well, the patent applications may be abandoned.

This 2.5-year time frame can actually be expanded to 3.5 years by using the one-year-on-sale bar as well (in the United States, companies have up to one year to file a patent application after introducing a product for sale to the marketplace); however, doing this would negate the ability to file for subsequent international patents. Read more about these new laws in Chapters 3 and 4, and work with corporate patent counsel and your PQM Team to develop a strategy that takes advantage of the most current laws.

ple suppliers will be expected. In part, bad habits have developed requiring price bids and competitive quotations, and in part, they want safety in multiple suppliers as a precaution. One supplier may go on strike, have internal production problems, get sold, or even go out of business or out of the product line. To these customers, multiple suppliers are critical to an uninterrupted supply of product.

Infringement

Infringement of your patents can have a negative effect on the department's sales and profits, but there can be a real pot of gold at the end of the rainbow. Granted, no one likes litigation, but with patent infringement, the stakes are much higher and the potential to recapture lost profits much greater.

There are several strategies when patents are being infringed. One of the more popular approaches for smaller companies' patents being infringed by larger companies is to let the infringement continue for

PROPOSED 2003 PATENT OFFICE RULES

Longer Pendency May Increase Infringement

The practical increase in pendency to more than three years under the new 21st Century Strategic Plan (as compared to the technical definition of the patent-pending period that begins with the examination request) may increase the incidence of patent infringement. The chief reason is that the subject matter in patent applications may now be held confidential for long periods before publication—possibly more than three years. A subsequent company beginning the development of the same technology during this time frame could be unaware of the long-delayed application and would find themselves infringing the earlier patent once it issues.

several years. The statute of limitations with patent infringement is six years. If the infringing party is knowingly infringing a patent over several years, and the patent holder can illustrate the amount of lost sales over those years, then the infringer could be liable for treble damages on the lost sales plus attorney's fees.

What's more interesting is that reports say that about 70 percent of all court cases involving patent infringement are awarded in favor of the patent holder. More important, it is reported that about 80 to 90 percent of all infringement cases are settled before they go to court, and an even higher percentage, 80 to 90 percent of those are settled in favor of the patent holder.

What this means to the marketing department is that protective laws are in place that allow you to recapture lost sales and revenue. It means that establishing a PQM system can serve the higher interests of the department and the corporation and is a cost effective means to do so.

Establishing a Patent Plan in Marketing

A corporation's PQM system in the marketing department is an excellent opportunity to obtain a marketing edge and provide substantial new revenue and profits to the corporation. The marketing department's patent development activities differ from other departments in that it is the one department that is usually closest to the customer. Its activities tend to be ones that are related to problems customers have with an existing product line as well as seeking out new related opportunities for the corporation.

The importance of the marketing department providing input into product development goes without saying. Without sales, the company cannot exist. Without continual improvement to the product line and identifying new patentable or patented technologies to license in, there will most likely be no future sales. Thus everyone in the corporation depends on the marketing department to do its job.

Goals

The chief goals of the PQM system in the marketing department are to seek out new problem-solving opportunities with the existing product line and to find new product opportunities as an adjunct to the existing line and patent them. In turn, these patents protect the corporation's sales and marketing efforts of the product line with a long-term revenue stream and profits.

Sales and marketing vice presidents, regional and local sales managers, product managers, technical support personnel, and customer and marketing support personnel all play a part in the department's PQM system.

Communication among these marketing department employees tends to be open and swift, allowing for a relatively prompt information flow. This process is conducive to employing a PQM system in the department and soliciting input from those who have intimate knowledge and experience with sales of products in a given marketplace, application, or customer. Identifying problems and opportunities is crucial to identifying new product development improvement and opportunities.

Those who repeatedly identify profitable opportunities in marketing tend to climb the corporate ladder quickly. So, being part of the PQM Team is a good opportunity to gain recognition and open up promotion opportunities. This kind of employee recognition only leads to the identification of other problematic areas and opportunities and new patentable improvement.

Similar to all departments, the PQM system in the marketing department must focus on quality opportunities and quality patents. Patents that will endure in the long run will ensure future sales for years to come. It would be unwise to spend time, money, and resources on a minor product improvement that will not provide sufficient sales or ROI. It is a primary responsibility of the management of this department to learn about and understand the value of increased market share versus the cost of patenting and the types of patentable opportunities. Marketing management cannot just assume that someone within the organization is going to automatically identify new opportunities and patent them on the department's behalf.

Implementing the Plan

In a TQM system, the marketing department becomes a primary source of information to the steering committee. In concert with TQM methodologies, the PQM system in the marketing department takes information and evaluates, then investigates potential product improvement and development opportunities.

There is one fundamental difference between the information sought out for TQM purposes and PQM purposes. TQM asks the marketing department to stay close to the customer and get information that will be helpful to determine how well the company is doing with the present product line and how it can enhance present products. PQM asks the marketing department to take it to the next level: To gather information that will determine how the company could augment the present product line and ultimately discover what is the greatest potential product of the future.

While enhancing a present product line is of value, it rarely has a long-term effect and is rarely protected by patents; however, when augmenting a product or product line, there tends to be a more long-term effect and patentability comes into play. A product may be augmented by a substantial improvement, and a product line may be augmented by either licensing in new related products (usually patented) or by creating new niche variations on existing ones, which too may be patented.

The major challenge of the marketing department is to make those innovative discoveries that will define the product's future or invent new products that may even replace the present product in the future. No company can be afraid to attack itself or else it will certainly lose its market share.

Generally speaking, marketing department meetings are held in one- to two-week time periods, which is adequate for PQM building. At these meetings, competitors' positions and advancements are discussed along with their new product improvements and releases. More important, the team discusses what it is doing to make greater advancements than its competitors or, at the very least, what it is doing to keep up.

The marketing department's PQM team is usually headed by at least one top-level marketing director or vice president. When new opportunities arise, the department's team creates a new project team to manage and implement the product evaluation and development plan.

The same team format may be used with the PQM system. In fact, the same TQM team members may likely be the best personnel to implement and manage the department's PQM system. PQM meetings may be added on as a simple adjunct to the existing TQM meetings. Thus it would require little extra effort from the team's routine activities.

Similar to other departments, before implementing PQM in the marketing department, all employees must have signed the company's patent protection documents, acknowledging confidentiality of the inventive matters to be discussed and developed, and of course, assigning their rights to the corporation. If this has not been completed, then this may be the first step in implementing a plan in the department. The corporation's legal counsel can prepare the documents.

Soliciting Inventive New Product Opportunities and Solutions

New opportunities in the marketing department can be solicited from a variety of sources, starting with individuals inside the department to

gathering information from sources outside. Primary sources for soliciting new opportunities for the marketing department are as follows:

- *Brainstorming sessions.* The department's PQM team meets and
  employs commonly used team techniques for brainstorming
  new concepts.

- *Management driven.* Directives from upper management to
  change, modify, or improve products to meet emerging market
  demands may be developed into patentable material.

- *Customer service department.* Lists of customer complaints tallied
  by the marketing department may reveal opportunities to augment existing products in order to fix existing problems.

- *Staying close to the customer, the end user.* Probably the best way
  to determine new innovation opportunities is by staying close
  to your customers and finding out what their future needs are.
  This is not always easy because many marketing departments
  are somewhat removed from the end user. They tend to deal
  only with major retailers and distributors and rely on their
  input instead. It can be a fatal error to rely on a distributor or
  retailer to tell you about future end user trends. This is one of
  your marketing department's fundamental responsibilities.

- *Staying close to distributors and retailers.* Some emerging trends
  can be tracked through them, including sales trends and, to a
  degree, consumer buying habits. Some secondary opportunities—the augmented product—may arise from the needs of
  the distributors and retailers.

- *Customer surveys.* Market surveys conducted with existing customers and potential customers can help point the direction of
  future product trends and opportunities.

- *Common sense.* Sometimes only common sense is needed in
  order to reveal exciting future opportunities. For instance, if
  something is being made in paper today, it's most likely going
  to be made in plastic soon. Or if a product is packaged in glass
  or aluminum, sooner or later it'll be plastic too.

111

- *Outside entities.* Outside sources should be encouraged to submit new license in opportunities to the department. This may be especially true if the outside entity is one that is close to the customer—the end user customer.

In marketing department PQM meetings, no idea or new product concept—no matter how far out it may appear—should be turned down. It is amazing how often some of the wacky concepts of yesterday have become the reality of tomorrow. Those concepts that seem too far-fetched should only be put on the back burner, and those that can have a more immediate impact are evaluated and pursued.

Assessment: Team Review

The assessment team for the marketing department's innovations must be led by those individuals who are experienced in the field and have demonstrated substantial future vision. All the right decisions must be made to ensure that the right innovations are pursued because these decisions are so important to the company's future revenue stream.

The marketing department's team would typically include qualifying members from outside the department as well. The most important outside member would be a top manager of the manufacturing department because of the importance of making certain that a new innovation or improvement to an existing innovation can be made cost effectively. It would be fruitless to proceed on a new innovation if the cost to manufacture was so high it couldn't be sold. The production processes also can't be arbitrarily changed without approval from the manufacturing department.

The primary assessment team members would most likely include the following:

- *Marketing department head.* Leads the evaluation team. This should be the top sales/marketing manager, for instance, a corporate vice president.

- *Marketing manager.* Provides marketing input based on his or her information sources and surveys.

- *Regional sales manager.* Provides more hands-on feedback from the field and must have an excellent pulse on current market trends and competitive positions.

- *Manufacturing manager.* Qualifies feasibility and cost effectiveness to manufacture.

- *Engineering manager.* Qualifies the feasibility and cost to engineer new improvements into existing products or the cost to engineer new innovations or licensed in products.

- *Legal counsel.* Qualifies patentability and scope.

- *Finance department.* Determines if the investment and payback can be justified.

The marketing department team is typically the largest because its influence overlaps into all other departments of the corporation. The importance of satisfying all aspects of developing a new improvement or entirely new innovation is inherent.

Other Contributors

There may be other experts who would participate in team reviews (e.g., to qualify health, safety, and legal considerations) who may come from inside or outside the corporation (e.g., a raw materials supplier, the FDA, an injection molding expert, machinists, and so on).

These persons are not considered contributors to the invention or part of the assessment team but are only providing information that the assessment team would use to evaluate functionality, the best technology to employ, or market potential. Inventive matter should not be disclosed to these entities unless absolutely necessary, which would require that they sign confidentiality agreements, including the release of all rights if a contributory discovery is made on their behalf.

Approval Systems

Upon gathering and assessing product improvement and new innovations, the team will either accept or reject the project. A consensus opinion should be required to pursue further development and to qualify if the project is a go or no-go, arrange test marketing, and ramp up. If there is no consensus, further assessment is required.

A decision to not patent an improvement does not necessarily mean that the project is abandoned. It may mean that patent protection would most likely not be broad enough to provide much protection. It may also indicate that the improvement is not of sufficient importance to affect a positive outcome on sales. The team may determine to pursue the new improvement without patent protection, because it represents a minor impact on sales and profits, providing it is easy and cost effective to pursue and implement.

CHAPTER 6

Managing Patents in the Engineering Department

After reading this chapter you will be able to

- Understand the value of fostering awareness of patent generation among the engineering staff

- Learn how to educate engineering staff in how to read patents

- Help engineering departments learn their responsibilities in terms of patent generation and design

- Understand how to design and implement an engineering patent plan

Engineers know all about patents, right? Interestingly, the answer is a resounding "no"!

Engineering is a technical profession. It is a discipline that applies science to problems and creates solutions to help humankind. Engineers can fall into various labels such as R&D professionals, researchers, scientists, product developers, and designers, but few engineers are inventors, and even fewer are knowledgeable of the patent process.

Engineering specialties include mechanical, manufacturing, industrial, biotech, chemical, electrical, civil, automotive, software, aeronautical, marine, mining, petroleum, and many, many more.

Engineers are trained to apply the laws of physics, engineering and scientific formulae, statistics and probability analysis, research methodologies, and the latest engineering tools to their craft. The fact is, engineers are trained to think *inside* the box.

Engineers and scientists have a technical skill set that naturally comes into play during the invention process, so these professionals *could* be prolific inventors if they receive the appropriate coaching and training. Without the training, most will remain as unfamiliar with the invention and patent process as a shoe salesperson.

This is where you, the Engineering Manager, come in.

Until universities start granting degrees in invention engineering, it will be the engineering manager's job to create the environment, procedures, incentives, and learning tools to help engineers and scientists become valuable contributors to the corporate patent portfolio. So just when you thought that patent management in the engineering department was old news, you're about to learn the value in reengineering the engineering department.

Invention Awareness

Engineers are taught in school about existing structures, materials, measures, mechanics, processes, and so on. They are not usually taught how to use their creativity to solve problems, but many do so naturally.

Innovative, inventive solutions to maximize a new product's quality with minimum manufacturing output are a prime objective. This must also be done with the consideration of startup costs and with long-term consistency. Engineers perfecting new products and processes with inventive solutions that may be protected by patents make the engineering department important to the corporation's future and stability.

It is also the engineer's responsibility to know what the present state of the art is in those processes, so that the newest, more cost-effective, high-productivity processes may be incorporated in the manufacturing department.

Kill NIH

For an engineering department to turn out high-quality, high-perform-ance products and solutions, it has to be open minded. Those open-minded corporations that do not have an NIH (not invented here) pol-icy and actively evaluate and employ outside technologies stand to be tomorrow's winners. At times pride can be a valuable trait in the corpo-rate environment; however, pride can also be one of the most destructive forces in a corporate environment!

NIH must be killed in the corporate environment, and the respon-sibility to kill it begins in the engineering department. You have an obli-gation to shareholders to generate sales and profits, and if they are being diminished because of an NIH attitude in the engineering department, it should be held accountable. Decisions to employ the best technolo-gies must be based on these innovations being efficacious, cost-effective, and showing long-term promise. Those individuals with an NIH atti-tude simply cannot slant decisions that will affect the future of the cor-poration and its shareholders.

No matter how brilliant an engineering department's employees may be, they simply cannot invent every new product and concept that comes along in a given field or industry. Adopting outside technologies and processes is fundamental to the future success of a product line or tantamount to success. The time savings involved with using other well-developed technologies also goes without saying. In this age of being fast, flexible, and focused in new product developments and getting to market fast, it becomes even more advantageous to consider outside technology sources.

Sometimes outside technologies may be purchased along with equipment or materials that are bought. Other times, the technologies can be licensed in or purchased outright from the owner. Regardless, broadening the corporate knowledge base with all available technologies, as well as emerging ones, is a wise policy to have in light of a rapidly changing world and inconstant consumer buying habits.

NIH attitudes must also be killed internally. The engineering department cannot be the sole source of invention within the corporation. Soliciting opportunities from all departments only makes sense. It broadens the corporate resources and tends to find new opportunities that would otherwise not be discovered. This is particularly true when a corporation's engineering department is not focused on the all-powerful end user. We say all-powerful because the end user—the primary buying influence—must be satisfied before all others. Without it, there will be no product pull through.

Causes and Conditions That Breed NIH

What causes NIH? It's human nature to develop a personality of laziness and resistance to change, especially in a work environment that charts employees' performance by how close to 8:00 a.m. they arrive, and how close to 5:00 p.m. they leave. If there is no incentive to change, break the mold, or take a risk, then the stage is set to develop NIH.

Uncover these symptoms of or excuses supporting the NIH syndrome, and you can start to address the underlying cause:

- I've done it like this for 20 years, and it's worked just fine. There's no need to change now. As the saying goes: "If it ain't broke, don't fix it."

- I'm retiring in 2 years. Why would I want to champion a risky new outside project? If it fails, I could get fired and lose my pension.

- I'm pulling down the big bucks to run a top-rate engineering department. If I have to suggest that we license in a key product or technology, it will suggest that I'm incapable of getting performance out of my own engineering group.

- It's too much trouble to work through the licensing process just to get a new product or technology. I'm hungry, it's late, so let's just forget it.

IN THE REAL WORLD

Engineers Are Not Inventors

Contrary to what intuition would lead us to believe, fewer than 2 percent of U.S. engineers and scientists will become inventors or patent holders in any given year.

A Plunketts' Engineering & Research Industry Statistics report showed a U.S. employment base of 3,369,400 scientists and engineers in 1997. A separate labor report of U.S. scientists and engineers showed 1.3 million science and technology professionals employed in basic, materials, and applied research, and an additional 1.9 million employed engineers (about 3.2 million combined). By contrast, the U.S. Patent Office statistics for 1999 show:

Total Patents Issued: 153,489 (about 115,000 [75 percent] to corporations)

Patents of U.S. Origin: 83,908 (about 63,000 [75%] to corporations)

Only 3 out of the top 10 patent-receiving companies in 1999 were American: IBM, Motorola, Lucent Technologies Inc.

Bottom line: On average, fewer than 1 in 50 engineers and scientists employed in the United States will receive a patent in any given year, or only 1.8 percent of practicing U.S. engineers and scientists.

Source: 1999 SETAT employment report, National Science Foundation data, and the U.S. Census Bureau, Statistical Abstract of the United States, Volumes 1995 through 2000, and U.S. Patent and Trademark Office.

- If we even *look* at product or technology suggestions from the outside, we're exposing ourselves to a possible lawsuit. Therefore, we need to put up a legal gauntlet so it only looks like we're open to outside technologies.

Almost every one of these symptoms is a result of selfishness, ego, hiding incompetence, or looking for excuses so one can continue to be lazy. There is absolutely no place for this individualistic attitude in a PQM environment, and in fact, this one dangerous affliction can do more to unravel an effective PQM program than any other factor.

Engineers as Part of PQM

The engineering department has the most dynamic PQM opportunity of all the departments. Because it tends to be at the hub of new product development and corresponding manufacturing processes, more responsibility is placed on it to engineer new products and solutions.

Traditionally, engineers in a TQM system are concerned with making incremental improvements. Today's challenges to the engineering department go beyond incremental improvements and include that of making new discoveries and creating new opportunities. Those engineers who excel in inventing valuable new products, improvements, and processes play an important part in the future of the corporation.

Engineering also plays a key role in the PQM teams in other departments throughout the corporation. In one regard, they are important qualifiers to the other departments, ensuring that low-productivity processes are not pursued, nor are products that may be costly to produce or tend to break easily. The engineering department can also guide and make recommendations to the other departments, for instance the marketing department, so that they may pursue products or improvements that are based on using certain processes consistent with the manufacturing department's present or future manufacturing methods.

Similarly, the engineering department may guide one of the other departments, such as manufacturing, so that new processes or improvements to existing processes it may want to consider will not sacrifice product quality or performance. As we well understand, manufacturing cannot drive sales without the danger of converting the existing product line into a generic product line and possibly losing all innovative sales advantages.

Patenting in the Engineering Department

The patent types that would be generated from the engineering department overlap into those patent types affecting the marketing and manufacturing departments; however, engineers should have a much more thorough understanding of these terms and their applications, as patent development becomes a more important part of their job responsibilities.

Invention Education: How to Read a Patent

By definition, a patent specification and description of the invention must provide sufficient information such that one skilled in the art (an engineer, perhaps) would be able to duplicate the results.

What patent information an engineer or scientist should read, and what information they should endeavor to extract from a patent, will depend on the objectives set forth by the engineering manager. Some managers will want the engineers to primarily study the description of the invention, possibly to learn more about the competitor's invention background. Other managers will want engineers to study every patent issued to the company's competitors, including invention background, claims, related patents, and drawings.

Engineering journals and science and technology textbooks all provide new and informative information of interest to engineers and scientists, but even the newest journals and books provide old data compared to weekly issued patents.

If engineers wish to remain on the cutting edge of a particular technology, and to remain a valuable knowledge resource to the company, they should know what new technologies and products are being patented. From this knowledge base, the engineers and scientists can learn the state of the art from these new patents and leap to the next evolution of the particular technology. The information will also give the engineers and scientists ideas to improve or design around the newly issued patent.

Product Patents

Those concepts that fall into the product patent group developed by the engineering department include new products, devices, and apparatuses used in the product line and define the specific unique, novel, and useful elements and attributes. They may encompass an individual product, apparatus, or device or an entire group of products. For engineers, they tend to be easily grasped concepts.

Method of Use or System Patents

These patents directly relate to making products people friendly and easy to use. This should be of particular interest to engineers, especially those involved with ergonomics. If there is any particular downfall to engineers, however, perhaps it may be that engineering as taught in universities, and incorporated in corporate America, does not seem to prioritize making products easy to use and people friendly. Engineering in our present-day society tends to be more structural and materials oriented, geared toward manufacturing and the related processes. It is, in fact, uncommon that engineering reaches the end users and truly takes their needs into consideration.

To engineers, systems patents define unique methods in which products are used. Patents may not be obtained on commonly used products and components, but when they are used in a novel, useful, and unique method, patentablity is possible. One or all of the components may be prior art as long as the outcome of the combined use is novel and unique. Think in terms of efficiency, effectiveness, and convenience for the end user and you're thinking in terms of systems patents.

Many electronics were brought to us by engineers, such as the VCR and the computer, but the people-friendly concepts invented by Sony and Apple made them easy to use, and frankly, easy to sell as well. It takes a fairly creative individual to envision future thinking opportunities and to solve the associated problems, but with practice it can be done. There is no one better to do this than an engineer—one who knows how to design and incorporate the best attributes based on current processes and materials.

Systems patents tend to point the engineering department in the right direction for future product development opportunities as well. They help turn the focus away from present-day manufacturing processes and dealing with what is already known and toward creating new products that customers will want to buy in the future. The corporation's survival depends on this approach.

We know that systems patents represent one of the greatest opportunities for businesses and the marketing department, but they also represent one of the best opportunities for the engineering department to follow through and make it happen. Maybe marketing doesn't know exactly how to do it, but their input as to what will sell with the customer can help steer engineering efforts in the right direction.

Improvement Patents

The very nature of the engineering department puts it in a perfect position to make a substantial number of product and process improvements that can be protected by improvement patents. Many improvements made by engineering may be patentable, but the real challenge is pursuing only those quality improvements that are worth the monetary and time investment. It really doesn't matter how you categorize what an improvement patent is, what's important is whether action is taken when opportunities arise and the corporation's intellectual property interests are protected.

It is important that product engineers understand that improvements to their existing product line or systems that qualify as being novel, unique, and useful may be patented by anyone outside the corporation. A customer-oriented engineering department must therefore always strive to set the standard for future product improvements, or else someone outside the corporation will. When those entities outside the corporation have developed new, improved, efficacious technologies, the smart engineering department will quickly adopt them by licensing in, thus reducing the time to develop and test alternate technologies, which may or may not be proved.

Process Patents

Process patents in the corporation tend to focus on internal manufacturing processes. In many corporations, perfecting internal manufacturing processes is the central focus of the engineering department. There's good reason for this: Highly efficacious manufacturing processes are instrumental in a corporation's ability to be profitable and successful.

Efforts aimed at improving and patenting internal processes should never be abandoned; however, there must be a balance between customer-driven innovations and improvements and internal processes. If the development of internal processes makes a product line so generic with such a narrow focus that it cannot be modified and improved, it will continue to lose market share to those product lines that are more adaptable to change and that can satisfy emerging trends.

Process patents can also be a valuable tool to overcome another emerging danger. At times, companies maintain certain manufacturing processes as closely guarded trade secrets; however, if an outside entity files a patent application that covers that trade secret, the company can lose its rights to the patent. In other words, the company holding the trade secret would be forced to license it from the new patent holder, regardless of how long the product had been in prior use. There have been several court case precedents on these kinds of actions. Obviously, the negative impact such a scenario could have on the corporation, the shareholders, the engineering department, and the engineers themselves is potentially disastrous. The best way to keep this from happening is by filing process patents before others do. Then you'll be in the admirable position of licensing them out instead.

A shift in focus toward becoming a more customer-driven, innovation-oriented corporation must be accompanied by cost-effective manufacturing processes. Engineering's responsibilities broaden as they search for means to satisfy both the customer and the manufacturing department.

Design Patents

Design patents refer only to the ornamental design but may become a minor part of the engineering department's arsenal of patents. More and more pressure is being put on engineers to incorporate superior aesthetics when designing new products and improvements. From this perspective, design patent protection may accompany utility patent protection. Design patents can help preserve that original, proprietary, or new look and have a positive effect on marketability.

Even though the department's focus is principally that of engineering new products and improvements covered by utility patents that afford superior patent protection, there are times when a simple design patent may serve the desired purpose (e.g., to preserve a certain proprietary appearance). But generally speaking, engineers will not be design-ing for aesthetics first and should strive to secure utility patent protec-tion whenever possible.

Engineering's Responsibilities

In a rapidly changing world, the focus of the engineering department also changes. In the early 1900s, businesses were manufacturing driven, led by the creation of Henry Ford's production line. In the 1930s, the transition to being sales driven was led by General Motors, which broadened product lines and offered assorted colors. It was not until quality management systems were adopted in the latter part of the twentieth century that business began to shift to being customer driven.

Where is your corporation's engineering department's focus? Unfortunately, many of today's engineering departments have been based on antiquated business structures and are still focused on being manufacturing driven or, at best, sales driven. Companies that will experience the highest degree of success in the twenty-first century are those that have a strong customer focus in their engineering depart-ments.

Designing for the End User

Engineering departments tend to be shielded from the end users, so valuable information on trends, user tendencies, and buying habits may be slow in reaching the engineering department. We cannot overlook the basic fact that the most important customer of all—the most impor-tant buying influence—is the end user. Although some companies may say they focus on being customer driven, this focus usually pertains to internal operations and customer support services. Very few companies take it to the next level and focus their product innovations and engineering on being customer driven. For those companies that see customer-driven innovation as the driving force behind new products and improvements, opportunities will abound. Patents can protect these new inventive opportunities.

One of the best ways for engineering to identify new inventive opportunities is from feedback from the marketing department (as suggested by TQM systems). Another source is from an internal R&D department (sometimes supplied by marketing, sometimes secured on its own), which may fall under the management of the engineering or marketing department. A third source of identifying inventive opportunities is from the engineers themselves, in particular, those who tend to work with customers on technical service calls in support of the marketing department. All of these approaches have their benefits; all have their downfalls.

Marketing people tend to have some of the best big picture feedback on market trends. Well-trained R&D personnel who work hands-on with end user customers may be able to ask better questions, get to the root of present problems, and project future opportunities. An experienced engineer may be able to identify present problems, but because his or her experience is based on a present knowledge base, can this person really solve those problems, let alone discover and invent new opportunities?

Because it is difficult for customers to easily clarify their real needs, experience and a team effort are two of the best tools we can use to uncover these needs. By listening carefully to the big picture problems and opportunities presented by marketing, engineering departments can convert them into viable solutions. It is fairly uncommon that new improvements solving present-day problems and also new products are automatically invented by the engineering department. The spark usually begins elsewhere.

Where does your engineering department get its market data?

Being Aware of the State-of-the-Art

Engineering must also stay on top of competitive developments. It must be aware of new improvements competitors are releasing in the marketplace and the response they have received—positive or negative. Those new innovations that have been well-received are usually setting a new industry standard—the new state of the art.

A good example of this phenomena has been the industrywide shift in retail packaging from paperboard cartons into plastic pouches in many products such as cookies, fruit drinks, dried fruit products, grains, and so on. The perceived quality and value of the new pouch packaging is far superior, enhancing and improving sales potential. This trend will continue and spread throughout many other product lines in the coming years. It is the marketing department's responsibility to provide feedback on these kinds of emerging market trends, but the engineering department must use this information to prepare for the future now, instead of being forced to react tomorrow.

In this R&D type of function, your marketing department is one of your company's most important sources of securing competitive information and feedback for your department. A team effort between your engineering and marketing department should be an R&D task force that is continually qualifying the state of the art in your industry, so you may be in the leadership role.

Design-Arounds

At times, technologies have been developed by competitors or others that may not be available for license. This could be for several reasons: (1) the owner wants to keep it exclusive; (2) royalty rates are too high; (3) the licensor is difficult to deal with; or (4) the technology's patent protection is inadequate. All of these are good reasons to design around an existing technology.

Before starting out, you will want to have an in-depth understanding of the technology that is being designed around. Your legal counsel should first provide you with its opinion on the scope of the existing patent and give you guidance on which elements must be excluded (or perhaps in what combination they may be included) in your design-around efforts.

One of the key approaches to designing around existing patents is to ask the question, "What is the next generation?" If your department is assigned the task of designing around an existing technology, why not take it to the next level and invent that instead? Why not learn from the all-powerful end users and discover what they would really like to have—not today, but tomorrow, in the future.

Designing around existing patents can be one of the engineering department's greatest challenges, but it can be one of the most rewarding as well. It can point the corporation's product line in a dynamic new direction, represent new profit potential, and bring substantial recognition to the department.

Improving Manufacturing Processes, Striving for Zero Defects

The engineering department's focus in the manufacturing environment is to work with the manufacturing department to eliminate bottlenecks, increase productivity and output, and improve product quality. Raising production a single percentage point can be substantial. All the while, production processes beg to be geared toward the more generic, high-volume products, whereas customer product demands lead in a direction that is more specific, niche oriented, and with many variables.

Therein lies one of the challenges to all engineering departments. If your manufacturing department is oriented toward the high-volume, generic market, you're going to get "niched to death" by your competitors, and your market share will be on a permanent decline.

The use of automation creates new challenges in manufacturing, in that it may tend to restrict the ability to manufacture short-run niche products. Engineering departments that can solve these problems are setting the stage for some powerful patents. The engineering department's PQM strategy must reflect this realigned product and production development strategy that focuses more on being customer driven, with the end users' present and future needs in mind, and less on being manufacturing driven.

The engineering department assists manufacturing in finding new ways to decrease defects. This may include physical changes to production equipment, machinery and processes. This may also include making production lines more flexible and adaptable to making niche products by using new methodologies of handling and processing goods, information, and production data. The resultant patents can have a far-reaching impact on keeping others out of your newly created niche markets. After all, each mass-produced product started out as a niche product anyway. If you don't do it, one of your competitors will. It is your department's responsibility to protect these new market advances with patents.

Reducing Product Downtime and Changeover

Working with the manufacturing department to reduce downtime and changeover is another important responsibility of engineering. As markets turn away from high-volume generic products and more towards niches, downtime and changeover time can make a production facility more vulnerable or more valuable, depending on the action taken.

Inventive methodologies and processes developed by the engineering department to ensure smooth, fast transitions from one product to the next will be extremely valuable, if not essential, in order to meet marketing demands. This may include engineering's ability to develop new information processing systems and corresponding software. All of these methods and processes of improving changeover time can be patentable.

Similarly, if engineering can work to reduce maintenance requirements, productivity is also improved. Innovative systems and processes that either reduce maintenance or decrease the time required to maintain and repair equipment may be patentable.

Reducing Waste

First, waste reduction in manufacturing operations associated with raw materials and product fabrication is another primary responsibility of engineering. So is waste reduction caused by defective products or processes. It goes without saying: Solve a defect problem related to production and the waste is also eliminated.

Although it may be technically impossible to have zero raw material waste in some fabrication processes, how that waste is handled may be important. For instance, proprietary waste handling systems that reprocess and recycle raw material should reduce raw material costs and may be patentable. Patents could be a simple way to create a raw material cost advantage over competitors. In this fashion, you could end up profiting from the processing of your competitor's scrap.

We also know that waste generated by defective products has a huge negative impact on the cost of quality. The cost to rework or discard defective products represents additional handling and expense. Systems and methods to reduce defects, thus reducing their corresponding waste before it happens, can be highly desirable and patentable.

Safety

In every facet of engineering's activities, safety is a primary concern. Incorporating elements of safety in plant operations, equipment, and systems can improve profits by reducing insurance premiums. It also contributes to employees' positive state of mind, which affects productivity.

Engineering innovations that improve safety in plant operations may be patentable. This includes safety devices, novel manufacturing processes, and even new employee training and operating systems.

License In Technologies

Engineering must also consider licensing in patented technologies in its quest to develop and improve new products and improve manufacturing processes and safety. This may include patented machinery for manufacturing the product line, patented components, and raw materials,

PROPOSED 2003 PATENT OFFICE RULES

Engineers Get Greater Patent Responsibility

The new 21st Century Strategic Plan affects the engineering department, too.

Because of the likelihood of incredible increase in patent fees, on one hand, and the corporate drive to reduce budgets and become more efficient, on the other, engineers now have a new responsibility to consider.

In order to curb runaway patent costs while preserving and growing shareholder value, engineers have to be more selective and will have to sift out those bad or marginal concepts not worth investing in. It's no coincidence that this more responsible behavior is what the USPTO wanted to influence anyway. They wanted to change the behavior of those companies filing patent applications inundated with multiple inventions and innocuous, seemingly irrelevant subject matter. From now on, only those entities with money to burn will have such a luxury. But is this fair to the shareholders?

and licensed in processes and technologies that lower defects. It could also include licensed in trade secrets.

Licensing in also avoids the incredibly damaging consequences associated with patent infringement, if an already patented technology was used. Knowing you are using infringing technology and doing so anyway usually results in treble damages being awarded. Being aware of new emerging technologies and incorporating them into the corporation's operations is the responsibility of the engineering department.

The Engineering Department's Patent Plan

Adopting a PQM system in the engineering department should be considered a top priority. You are the ones who ultimately design the products and engineer the manufacturing of them. You have a responsibility to the corporation and its shareholders to protect all new, valuable discoveries with patents. Engineering also has a responsibility to protect the corporate assets against infringement of other patents and to be aware of emerging technologies. The engineering department plays an important part in the patenting activities of all departments, and present quality management systems will allow the PQM system employed in engineering to reinforce the efforts throughout the entire corporation. In fact, it may serve as the PQM ambassador to all other departments.

Goals

The chief goals of the PQM system in the engineering department are as follows:

- Identify, develop, and patent customer-driven concepts of the future.
- Improve manufacturing processes, systems, and safety, and protect them with patents.

- Work closely with the other departments to assist in developing their patentable concepts.

- Identify license in technologies and assist in their evaluation.

The engineering department's goals reflect a greater responsibility to integrate patenting activities into the corporation. Working with other employees in a team environment can produce some fairly remarkable results. This is particularly true when identifying customer-driven opportunities. The PQM system in the engineering department can and should solicit input from those who have intimate knowledge and experience with end user customers.

The same holds true for new manufacturing equipment and processes. Asking production department managers and employees for their input in your new patented technologies is almost always well received.

Last, engineering employees building the corporation's patent portfolio will receive significant recognition. Employee recognition encourages others to contribute and will serve to establish a successful PQM system. A PQM system that develops a portfolio of quality patents affects marketing, production, and all departments.

Implementing the Plan

This engineering PQM team should be headed by a top-level manager, preferably the same manager who heads the department's TQM management team. The same TQM management team is most likely the best team to implement and manage the PQM system and to appoint project teams to develop patented improvements and technologies. This work can usually be accomplished in your meeting activities.

The initial PQM objective would be to identify existing patent opportunities on present projects. Another objective is to evaluate and then adjust the focus of the department to a more customer-driven entity as desired. A third objective would be to implement a system to work more closely with other departments to assist them in identifying existing or new patentable or license in opportunities.

Similar to all other departments, employees must have signed the company's patent protection documents, acknowledging confidentiality of the inventive matters to be discussed and developed, and of course, assigning their rights to the corporation before participation. These documents should be prepared by the corporation's legal counsel.

Soliciting Inventive Opportunities and Solutions

Fortunately, soliciting inventive opportunities in the engineering department is not too difficult. Most of the opportunities will be problem-solving efforts for, or generated by, other departments. Proficient communications among the other departments then becomes the principal pipeline of opportunity.

Five ways to solicit inventive opportunities are as follows:

1. *PQM Management Team generated.* The team addresses immediate and emerging opportunities of which it is aware. Brainstorming sessions can expand on the possibilities.

2. *Management driven.* Directives come from upper managers, who have identified emerging opportunities with new products, improvements, and technologies that could be licensed in.

3. *Manufacturing department.* As bottlenecks and more serious production and potential safety problems are identified, engineering is best suited to get involved and tackle these issues.

4. *Marketing department.* It should have the best understanding of customer needs, problems, and at times emerging opportunities.

5. *The augmented product and the potential product.* A change in mind-set is needed from thinking in terms of simple improvements to higher-level concepts that either augment or strive toward achieving the potential product.

Engineering must always keep in mind that it will be looking at most of these opportunities from a technical viewpoint, which is right at the heart of patenting, but the other departments may instead be talking in broad generalizations that may not be patentable. For instance, if another department generalized, "It would be better if the machine ran more quietly," it would then be up to engineering to invent a way to do exactly that. Some ideas or suggestions you encounter may even seem strange, but it's important to listen to what is really being said and to analyze why these requests are being made. Usually there is some underlying influence or cause of a problem that is begging for your inventive solution.

Assessment: Team Review

The team approach to assessing which patenting opportunities are pursued in the engineering department will most likely need to be approved by the departments they affect. For instance, it goes without saying that engineering can't arbitrarily change product performance without approval from the marketing department. Similarly, new manufacturing processes cannot be introduced without the manufacturing department signing off, and also the marketing department if the new process may in any way affect the product line.

The primary engineering department assessment team members would typically include the following:

- *Department head.* The leader of the evaluation team would most likely be one of the department's top managers.

- *Project leader.* The engineer who headed up the development project must be included in the team.

- *Corresponding department manager.* A manager from the corresponding department that is affected by the patented matter should be a part of the decision-making process. For instance, this could be a national sales manager or a plant manager.

- *Legal counsel.* The qualification of patentability and scope will be determined.

- *Finance department.* This department determines if the investment and payback can be justified.

There may be others who would participate in team reviews. For instance, a safety supervisor would give input into safety-related innovations or a trainer into training-related methods and systems.

Other Contributors

The engineering department would typically use a host of outside materials and parts suppliers to qualify various aspects. For instance, raw materials, software and chip components, and machining tolerances are usually best determined by outside experts.

These persons are not considered contributors to the invention or a part of the assessment team, but they would provide information so that the assessment team could evaluate the functionality or best technology and inventive potential. Inventive matter should not be disclosed to these entities unless absolutely necessary. Before disclosure, they must sign a confidentiality agreement that includes the release of all rights if a contributory discovery is made on their behalf.

Approval Systems

Upon assessment of the various aspects of a patentable opportunity, the team will either accept or reject the idea. New opportunities should meet everyone's approval as a consensus decision. Without a consensus, further investigation and consideration should be given to resolve conflicting issues.

Lack of approval of pursuing a patent on a new engineering discovery does not necessarily mean that the project is abandoned, but that there are some unresolved or unqualified issues. It could simply mean that there is not enough protection or payback on the money and time investment to file and prosecute a patent application. Many patenting opportunities in the engineering department will be the result of ongoing projects and problem-solving requests anyway. Thus the decision to patent or not may not be relevant to the development and implementation of the project.

Engineers as Ambassadors

Contrary to most present-day operating conditions and corporate structures, the engineering department in the PQM system is being asked to be an ambassador of a sort. It can—in fact, should—be instrumental in the development of most all of the new technologies embraced within the corporation, whether they are developed internally or licensed in.

We know that the engineering department's primary job is to work with the other departments to solve problems, make improvements, and so on. With innovation and PQM being so important to the future of a corporation, this role should be expanded. The new system commands that innovations be customer driven and qualified across the corporation. From this perspective, the engineer's role becomes more ambassadorial, and frankly more enjoyable, than ever before.

CHAPTER 7

Managing Patents in Manufacturing and Operations

After reading this chapter you will be able to

- Understand how quality improvement can lower costs in terms of patents

- Understand patents versus trade secrets and how process and method patents can influence the bottom line

- Learn the benefits of improved processes: eliminate bottlenecks, reduce defects, reduce product downtime and changeover, reduce waste, and improve safety

- Understand how to develop and implement a patent plan for the manufacturing department

The primary objectives of manufacturing operations are to improve product quality and productivity, lower manufacturing costs, and reduce defects, rework, and downtime. The sum total of these efforts improves profitability and overall customer satisfaction.

Innovative, inventive solutions play an important part in accomplishing these prime objectives. When inventive solutions are protected by patents, and at times trade secrets, they enhance the corporation's future profitability and ensure product life longevity.

Improving Quality, Lowering Costs

The quality management paradigms in most of corporate America utilize the most advanced methods of controlling manufacturing processes

so that production is consistent and stable, defects and rework are min-
imized, output is maximized, and the cost of goods is low. It is also about
reducing downtime and changeover time as a manufacturing facility
strives to be fast, flexible, and focused. Thus quality management not
only capitalizes on being a low-cost producer in an existing market but
capitalizes on higher-profit niche markets as well.

Niche marketing is particularly important in twenty-first century
marketing efforts because every generic product that hasn't been niched
will be sooner or later. So why not your corporation? If you're not in a
position to divide your product group into niches, then a competitor
certainly will. Building and preserving the ability to rapidly change over
production to manufacture a multitude of different niche products can
put your company at a competitive advantage within your industry segment.

Quality-managed manufacturing plants, by their very nature, have
abundant opportunity to make a positive impact on the corporation's
future. It only makes sense to protect those achievements by patents or
by closely guarded trade secrets.

Patents versus Trade Secrets
Patents for Your Process

We know that process patents generally refer to manufacturing processes
and may be accompanied by machine patents. Machine patents are not
normally created in a manufacturing department, but rather in your
engineering department, or by appointed suppliers; however, process
patents can offer broad protection to your manufacturing department
and represent valuable patenting opportunities.

You are certainly aware of the competitive advantage a proprietary
process may provide with just 1 percent cost savings over competitors.
It could represent millions in profits, revenue for expansion or equip-

ment upgrades, or it could even mean the difference between staying in or going out of business.

Inventing and developing superior processes is crucial to every prosperous business. Think about inventive processes like Eli Whitney's cotton gin and the cost of blue jeans if cottonseeds were manually extracted? Think about the invention of pasteurization and its value to humankind. New processes and their accompanied patents often offer significant improvements to the quality of life. Processes such as high-speed manufacturing, automated, and robotic processes all lend themselves to patent protection.

Successful new products and new product improvements will rely heavily on cost-effective production in order to realize market penetration and sustained sales. The manufacturing department is going to be relied on to purchase new equipment, or make changes and modifications to existing equipment, in order to produce the new product. Thus proprietary processes and patenting opportunities may abound.

Methods Patents

Similar to process patents, new methodologies may also be patented. Where process patents are generally related to machinery, including computers, their use and related processes, methods, and systems patents relate to new ways in which people use or handle an item or material. Some examples of method patents include:

- *Patent No. 5,498,162.* Method for demonstrating a lifting technique (how to lift a box from the floor)
- *Patent No. 5,960,411.* Method and system for placing a purchase order via a communications network (otherwise known as Amazon.com's method for one-click ordering online)

This may include methods in handling merchandise, or methods of processing it, or even paperwork. More recently, some of these new patents have overlapped into an area that includes methods employees use to monitor processes and methods to improve training.

Trade Secrets

Trade secrets in the manufacturing arena are quite common. Tightly held, they can be more powerful than patents. Patents expire in 20 years, but trade secrets can go on indefinitely. The key is whether they can be closely held because once they're known by others, such as your competitors, there will be no more protection.

Maintaining manufacturing trade secrets can be very difficult if not impossible. Employees in an industry tend to stay in that industry. Workers who are laid off at one company will usually seek similar work

IN THE REAL WORLD

Patent Manufacturing Methods

NASA developed and patented a Method of Fabricating Composite Structures. This system, developed at NASA's Marshall Space Flight Center (MSFC), involves the fabrication of high-strength, low-weight laminated structures. The process has resulted in 15 to 40 percent weight savings, a critical attribute for aerospace and aircraft components. At the same time, 5 to 25 percent cost savings have been recorded in production programs!

This process has earned NASA U.S. patent number 5,084,219. Because NASA has proven the financial benefit, as well as the commercially competitive product attributes that result from using its new manufacturing process, it is making this patent available for license. In addition to the already documented savings, licensing represents yet another source of possible revenue for NASA, illustrating the significant value that process patents can deliver to the organization.

at a competitor's facility. Thus it is common for employees to talk about the previous employer's manufacturing processes. It happens all the time.

Generally speaking, the fewer the personnel who know the trade secret, the easier it will be to keep and vice versa. Any intent on behalf of the corporation to closely guard trade secrets should be accompanied by an employee trade secret program. The corporation's legal counsel can prepare the documents.

Trade secrets may at times also be securely maintained in other ways, for instance, in locked facilities and black boxes, and even through company policies. For years Xerox maintained its proprietary plain paper copying process by keeping it in a black box inside the copier, which was only accessible by an authorized service person who had the appropriate key. Xerox further protected its technology by using a key and lock system that was not available to ordinary locksmiths. Also, Xerox didn't sell its machines; they were available for lease only.

The obvious alternative to a difficult-to-maintain and monitor trade secret program is patent development. After all, it is relatively uncommon that a technology will last for more than 20 years, and if it does, it would be subject to improvement anyway. The improvements often become more valuable than the original patent.

Improving Processes

The first stages of installing a TQM system usually begin in the manufacturing department and quickly become the primary focus of the corporation's activities. What's more important is that statistical process control (SPC) taught by TQM methodologies is important to developing and patenting superior processes. Nothing could make inventive matter more patentable and less vulnerable to scrutiny than to be supported with SPC documentation.

Once SPC is established and processes are controlled, monitoring and improving them represents an outstanding PQM opportunity in the manufacturing department. There are numerous areas of significant value that can propel productivity and profits upward.

Before you embark on patenting ventures, however, we would like to introduce a word of caution before outlining possible manufacturing processes that you may consider patenting. If you believe that you can patent a particular process, keep in mind that your competitor may have the same thought, only one of you will earn a patent on the invention. So, before heavy investment is made in any new or novel manufacturing process—let alone the preparation of a patent on the process—make sure that your patent or corporate counsel completes a patent search and determines that you would not be infringing others' manufacturing process patents.

Eliminating Bottlenecks

In most manufacturing operations, relieving bottlenecks is a primary, ongoing objective. Using creative approaches to relieving bottlenecks can have a significant effect on improving productivity and output. A single 1 percent rise would be considered substantial if no other changes had to be made in a production line.

Bottlenecks may be relieved by employing new processes and machinery or handling equipment. This may be achieved by using automation, which usually reduces handling, or new methodologies and systems that reduce touches or manufacturing steps. Bottlenecks may also be relieved by employing a new methodology or routing system. All of these applications may be patentable.

Reducing Manufacturing Defects

Striving for zero defects is a goal of most companies. As manufacturing operations find new ways to decrease defects, they also find new patenting opportunities. These opportunities may include physical changes made to production equipment, machinery, and processes. They may also include new methodologies of handling and processing goods, information, and production data. Even an SPC system that helps anticipate changes in production controls that can have a negative future impact on production may be patentable.

New patented or licensed in technologies can also be used to reduce manufacturing defects. This may include patented machinery used to manufacture the product line, patented components and raw materials, and licensed in processes and technologies that lower defects. It could also include licensed in trade secrets.

Reducing Downtime and Changeover

Reducing downtime and changeover is another facet of manufacturing that can have a dramatic impact on productivity and output. High-volume manufacturing processes tend to focus on high-volume generic products, but modern history tells us that more and more generic products are being divided into niches. If you don't believe it, just look back a couple of decades ago when only a few body styles were offered by the major automakers. Today, every automaker offers dozens of body styles and variations just to stay in business: compact, small-, medium- and large-sized cars; two, three, and four doors; a few pickup truck varieties; SUVs; vans; and many others, like sports cars and convertibles.

Changeover time is a critical factor concerning production output. To lose just a single production hour in a shift can be extremely costly. A single hour lost during an eight-hour shift represents a roughly 16 percent decrease in output. Sometimes changeover times further magnify the decrease in productivity via the scrapping of defective product when adjusting machinery for the new output.

Smooth, fast transitions from one product to the next are essential in order to complement modern manufacturing processes and marketing demands. This is accompanied by the importance of having reliable information in order to change over quickly with a minimum amount of scrap. Mechanical or physical means and processes of improving rapid changeover time can be patentable. So may information processing systems and their corresponding software.

Similarly, downtime resulting from normal maintenance requirements, refilling processes, and so on that can be shortened by new innovations and processes that may be patentable. Obviously the more difficult downtime challenges would be those that are unforeseen or caused by unforeseen causes, such as power outages; however, new methodologies to foresee potential problems that would cause breakage or downtime may be desirable and patentable.

Reducing Waste

Just like striving for zero defects, standard economic principles strive for zero waste. There are two types of waste; first is the natural waste experienced in a given manufacturing operation typically associated with raw materials and product fabrication; second, there is waste caused by defective products or inconsistent processes.

In many manufacturing operations it is technically impossible to have zero raw material waste if products or components are part of a cutout or fabrication process; however, what's done with the waste is important. Is it reprocessed or recycled, or is it simply discarded? How can raw material waste be reduced? If discarded, can it be reconstructed back to some usable form? Or can the raw material be reshaped into a different form or configuration to give a cutout a lower waste factor?

Small, incremental decreases in raw material waste may result in substantial increases in output and profitability. For instance, waste is considered as an expense, a cost to do business. If waste were reduced and converted into sellable merchandise, the swing in profitability could be substantial. Such a process not only cuts out the negative cost of handling waste, it generates profit instead.

Waste caused by the errant manufacture of defective products can be a disaster. First it has a huge negative impact on the cost of quality. Once a defective product is in the hands of a customer, it represents a negative experience and brings into question whether the customer would want to purchase the product again. Second, the product will be returned, perhaps reworked or thrown out, all of which represent additional handling and expense. Systems and methods to reduce defects either before or after discovery can be highly desirable and patentable.

Safety

Although making a plant's environment safer may not have a direct relationship to profitability, innovations that improve the operating safety in a plant can have an indirect impact. They can have a positive impact on insurance claims, thus reducing premiums, or improve working conditions and can have a positive impact on the state of mind of employees, thus potentially raising quality and improving output.

Again, many aspects of physically improving a plant's safety in its operations may be patentable, whether they are new safety devices or manufacturing processes. New employee operating systems that improve safety may also be patentable. Altogether, a PQM system in the manufacturing department that focuses on processes, machinery, and methods patents can improve a corporation's market position and profitability.

Establishing a Patent Plan

A corporation's PQM system should be considered an excellent opportunity to boost employee morale in the manufacturing department. After all, these are the people who physically make the products in the first place. This is where the hard work is done and where managers and employees often do not get the recognition they deserve. Quality management systems build teamwork. PQM systems reinforce the teamwork concept and can build recognition for employee efforts, especially if formal employee innovation recognition programs, such as those outlined for the HR department in Chapter 9, are implemented by the organization.

Goals

The chief goals of any patent-driven system in the manufacturing department are to improve the manufacturing processes, systems, and safety, which in turn should have a positive impact on product quality, productivity, and profitability.

Manufacturing managers, maintenance personnel, and many hands-on employees tend to have a good understanding of production processes. Streamlining, improving, and perfecting these processes with new innovations that can be protected with quality patents is a chief objective.

Production management and employees also tend to work well together as a team. This attribute is conducive to employing a PQM system in the department and soliciting the input from those who have intimate knowledge and experience in a given process or with the related machinery. Asking employees for their contribution to develop new patented technologies is almost always well received. Patented production methodologies are often invented and developed by a team of employees who are assigned to the project. Thus when the patent issues, it will have several co-inventors listed.

It's a well-known fact that when an employee is listed with his or her name on a U.S. patent, significant recognition and pride results. This employee is not only contributing substantially to the future profitability and security of the corporation, but has also become a part of history. His or her name will be permanently recorded in the annals of the U.S. Patent Office. This kind of employee recognition spurs on the employee to develop future contributions and will drive others to contribute as well. A successful PQM system can only add to building esprit de corps in a production department and to improving productivity and profits.

A PQM system in the production department must focus on the quality of the patents that will be developed. It would be counterproductive to spend time, money, and resources on minor advances in technology that will not provide payback on the investment. From this perspective, ROI is important. It is a primary responsibility of the managers of this department to learn about and understand the value of various gains that may be made in productivity, as well as the associated costs to develop and patent.

Implementing the Plan

With TQM, production processes and new improvements are discussed in management team meetings on a regular basis, usually weekly. This team is usually headed by a top-level manager from the production department. When certain production-related opportunities arise, the production management team may create a new project team to manage and implement the plan.

The same team format may be used with the PQM system, including the members of the same TQM management team. They are most likely the best-placed personnel to implement and manage a PQM system. This can usually be accomplished with little extra effort from the team's day-to-day activities.

Before implementing PQM in the manufacturing department, all employees must have signed the company's patent protection documents, acknowledging confidentiality of the inventive matters to be discussed and developed, and of course, assigning rights on those inventions to the corporation. If this has not been completed, this may be the first step in implementing a plan in the department. The HR department will have the appropriate employee forms.

Soliciting Inventive Opportunities and Solutions

There are several good methodologies to solicit inventive opportunities and solutions from managers, employees, and other departments. Generally speaking, managers will be thinking more in terms of improving productivity, whereas employees will think in terms of solving continual problems.

Five excellent methods to solicit inventive solutions are as follows:

1. *Suggestion box.* The same method used by employees soliciting their suggestions for plant improvements can be used in the PQM system.

2. *Brainstorming sessions.* Existing TQM production and project teams can employ commonly used team techniques to brainstorm and propose new concepts.

3. *Management driven.* Directives from upper management to change, modify, or improve certain aspects of production or safety requirements that may be developed into patentable material.

4. *Customer complaints.* Lists of customer complaints tallied by the marketing department almost always reveal solid opportunities for improvement. Evaluating these lists may reveal inventive opportunities for the department.

5. *The augmented product.* In concert with the marketing and engineering departments, new improvements may be desired for existing products, or it may be desirable to introduce new complementary products to the existing line; however, production processes and methods may not be in place, thwarting the new product's production. Inventive solutions from the manufacturing department may be the key to success.

No idea or invention, no matter how extreme it may appear, should be shunned or turned down. Employees must not be shut down or ridiculed for their thoughts and ideas because this can deter them from sharing future inspiration; however, only the cream at the top should be pursued.

Assessment: Team Review

The team approach to determining which opportunities and solutions may be pursued will typically include several parties and may also involve input from other departments. It goes without saying that production processes can't be arbitrarily changed without approval from other departments the changes may affect.

The primary assessment team members would most likely include the following:

1. *Department head.* The leader of the evaluation team could be a plant manager or general manager, or in a larger entity, it may include a corporate vice president of manufacturing.

2. *Shift supervisor.* This individual can give valuable input into the ability to implement new processes and systems.

3. *Maintenance supervisor.* This individual is usually the one who must install new devices and apparatuses. He or she must qualify the ease of installation and ongoing maintenance afterward.

4. *Legal counsel.* This person is responsible for determining qualification of patentability and scope.

5. *Finance department.* Determines if the investment and return can be justified.

6. *Human Resources department.* Will need to develop, implement, and manage employee invention assignment forms and employee recognition programs.

There may be others who would participate in team reviews: a safety supervisor would give input into safety-related innovations; a union steward may need to validate certain production changes or modifications; a marketing vice president may need to qualify changes that could affect sales.

Other Contributors

Aside from evaluating the inventive matter, specialists in various fields, inside and outside the corporation (such as a raw materials supplier, injection molding expert, machinists, and so on), may also be required to qualify certain aspects. These persons are not to be confused as contributors to the invention or part of the assessment team. They would typically be providing information that only the assessment team would use to evaluate the functionality or best technology and inventive potential. It is important that inventive matter is not disclosed to these entities, or if it is absolutely necessary to do so, that they sign confidentiality agreements including the release of all rights if a contributory discovery is made on their behalf.

Approval Systems

Upon gathering and assessing the various aspects of an opportunity, the assessment team will either accept or reject it. It's best that a new opportunity meet with everyone's approval as a consensus decision. If there is not a consensus, further consideration should be given to the project in order to resolve the detrimental issue(s).

Nonapproval of pursuing a patent on a new discovery does not necessarily mean that the project is abandoned, it only means that there appear to be unresolved or unqualified issues. Certainly, if the team determined that a new discovery would be advantageous but would have only a minor effect on productivity and profit, it could be pursued and implemented, without pursuing a patent and without incurring the expense.

Controlling Intellectual Property Handled by Your Vendors

The manufacturing department (or purchasing, depending on the organization) will typically be responsible for procuring assembly components from outside vendors. These components are often custom-made for you and are manufactured to your specification. Further, many times these components are or will be covered by one or more of your patents.

It's important to establish ownership of your intellectual property at the onset of a vendor relationship. Because the vendor is the expert in various processes, it's not uncommon for a vendor to improve your product (sometimes at your request); however, if this improvement becomes part of your patentable matter, then the vendor has just become a co-inventor with *100 percent of the rights and privileges of ownership that you enjoy, without any further obligation to you.*

CHAPTER 8

Managing Patents in the Finance Department

After reading this chapter you will be able to

- Understand patent financial management and the role of the CFO

- Understand Financial Accounting Standards (FAS-142)— intangible assets and financial reporting requirements

- Learn how to budget patents, including the costs of obtaining patents and investing in protection against patent infringement

- Learn the art and science of patent valuation and how to establish a fair market value

Despite what may seem like an obscure connection between patents and the CFO, patent financial management is not only an important component to the enterprise PQM plan, but the CFO stands alone in being able to directly and immediately alter shareholder value based on how effectively he or she manages and reports patent value.

There was a time when the extent to which a financial manager's dealing with patents amounted to little more than authorizing payment of the patent attorney's bill. After all, the finance department manages bank accounts, accounts payable, taxes, and budgeting. Engineering and legal were the only departments charged with managing patents. Not anymore!

In the wake of the Enron collapse, CFOs join the top management echelon that are increasingly finding themselves under the microscope, being held accountable by shareholders, customers, and reporting agencies for their management practices and decisions. Profits and earnings per share (EPS) are now important metrics that should be incorporated into every PQM system.

Today, more than ever, the CFO is answerable for mishandling the company's purse strings. This has always been the case to some degree, but the combined effect of the new Financial Accounting Standards Board (FASB) requirements to separately report intangible assets and the inordinately high ratio of intangible asset value to market value creates a higher standard of practice to which CFOs everywhere will be held.

If you are a CFO of a company on the order of magnitude of, let's say, Cisco Systems, ask yourself how much time you spend on managing cash and tangible assets, as compared to the time you spend managing intangible assets. If your management time is split 90 percent on cash and tangible assets and 10 percent on intangible assets, you (and your shareholders) may be surprised to learn that 90 percent of your time is being spent managing about 25 percent of the company's market value!

To illustrate why it's becoming increasingly important for CFOs to aggressively pursue PQM, take a look at how heavily IP value contributes to market capitalization.

Exhibit 8.1 only illustrates a snapshot of two companies on a particular day, but it stands to reason that the inordinately high value attributable to intellectual property demands that you implement a plan that tracks, evaluates, and reports changes in IP value.

Even if you manage the finances of a $25 million company, the same rules still apply on a smaller scale. In fact, one way that the CFO can single-handedly grow the smaller company's earnings and asset base, along with its IP value, is to replace weak or nonexistent patent man-

EXHIBIT 8.1

Examples of Market Capitalization in Excess of Book Value

Company	Market Capitalization	Book Value (Shareholder Equity)	Excess (IP Value)	IP Value as a % of Market Value
Cisco Systems	102,310	27,120	75,190	73%
Microsoft	303,752	47,289	256,463	84%

Examples reported by Gartner Group and calculated at close of business on 3 October 2001 ($ millions)

agement systems with strong financial management policies that will fully exploit the financial contribution that patents can produce. It's now important to begin managing patents in addition to your more traditional CFO duties.

Patents Equal Income

Although the CFO must begin managing all forms of goodwill and other intangible assets such as trademarks, copyrights, trade secrets, and more, the emphasis in this chapter is on patents and their ability to generate cash, cut development budgets, and increase shareholder value.

In this chapter, we introduce you to the various issues related directly to patents, an overview of the new Financial Accounting Standards (FAS-142), and other emerging issues of importance such as the following:

- Asset creation versus cash flow
- Patent-related borrowing power and taxes

- Cost of patents: Investing in domestic and international patent protection
- Costs of litigation and patent infringement insurance
- Cost of intellectual property and asset management (IPAM) software
- Divesting or acquiring patent portfolios/patent-related assets

There are as many corporate financial strategies as there are CFOs. Not all of the considerations presented here will apply to all CFOs, but this overview will serve as a beacon that illustrates how the finance department integrates with other departments in an enterprise. It will also help you discover which patent-related policies or management practices should receive more of your attention than they are receiving now, based on liability reduction and value creation objectives.

FAS-142: Intangible Assets and Financial Reporting Requirements

FAS-142 is probably the most important new rule that mandates the CFO's heightened diligence in managing intellectual property. The new FASB Statement No. 142 (FAS-142), *Goodwill and Other Intangible Assets*, was issued on July 20, 2001.

FAS-142 supersedes APB 17, *Intangible Assets*, and it primarily directs the accounting methods that must be applied to goodwill and intangible assets subsequent to the date they were initially recognized. In short, the statement ends amortization of many intangible assets and makes it mandatory for companies to instead apply a complex impairment test to the assets.

Of course, there are exceptions to how FAS-142 applies to not-for-profit organizations, as well as to assets acquired after certain dates. Your accounting or tax professional will be able to advise you on the specifics of FAS-142 for your particular situation.

Patents Contribute to Increased Shareholder Value

In a January 2002 release regarding full year 2002, SBC Communications Inc. (NYSE: SBC) stated that it expected 2002 EPS performance to increase based in part on its implementation of FAS-142, which changes how companies account for amortization of goodwill and certain other intangibles. Under FAS-142, SBC will add $0.13 to $0.15 to full-year earnings per share, on both a reported and normalized basis, even if no other operational, sales, or financial performance changes occur. The effect of FAS-142 alone represents an almost 7 percent increase in earnings performance—all tied to the new reporting of intangible assets, including patents!

SBC is not alone. The chart below shows how Johnson Controls, Inc. is visualizing the benefits of reporting under FAS-142. It's certain that most companies will take a more serious look at the development and value enhancement of patents to maximize intangible asset (and shareholder) value.

Extracted From CONSOLIDATED STATEMENT OF INCOME

Johnson Controls, Inc. (NYSE: JCI), Reported January 2002

The Adjusted Earnings Per Share (EPS) for 2000 shows the EPS with the effect of FAS-142 applied, as compared to the actual 2000 EPS as reported. The increase shows the positive impact of applying FAS-142.

	Adjusted 2000	2000	Incr/(Decr)
Basic	$1.35	$1.16	$0.19
Diluted	$1.27	$1.10	$0.17

Source: SBC release, January 24, 2002

159

Wall Street analysts have indicated that EPS increases of 107 to 115 percent could immediately result from the changeover to financial reporting that incorporates FAS-142. The methods by which CFOs manage intangible assets clearly have a significant and direct impact on shareholder value.

Among the new requirements and guidance set forth in FAS-142, the following are the most significant changes from APB 17 as they may pertain to patents:

- Goodwill and intangible assets that have indefinite useful lives can no longer be amortized but rather will be tested at least annually for impairment.

- Intangible assets that have finite useful lives will continue to be amortized over their useful lives, but without the constraint of an arbitrary ceiling of 40 years.

- Additional financial statement disclosures about goodwill and intangible assets will be required.

While FAS-142 applies to a company's intangible assets across the board, the effect on how patents will be treated is of special interest. CFOs will need to review how they have historically accounted for the investment in a patent or the underlying technology development costs and carry forward the amortized investment to conform to the new requirements.

Further, if a determined price is paid for patents (or trademarks and copyrights), either individually or as a component of an acquired intellectual property portfolio, special attention should be paid to how these assets transition to the new impairment tests.

CFOs may have a particularly difficult time determining the value of a patent because attributing a specific value to each identified intangible asset is required. Many factors unique to patents must be considered in determining the reported value:

- Remaining life of a patent
- Value changes that result from decisions of a Patent Office reexamination
- Value changes that result from infringement, either defensively or offensively
- Loss of value if your issued patent is later declared invalid
- Value of a divisional patent based in part on the established value of the underlying patent

Currently, there is no single metric against which to gauge or determine a patent's value. Although some currently available analytic tools can help the CFO develop an objective value, the methodology and algorithms used in the computer modeling are anything but standardized, and valuations determined by consulting firms and valuation experts are fraught with subjectivity. (Various patent valuation tools are reviewed later in this chapter.)

Pinning an objective value on any patent can be controvertible. Nevertheless, you can expect the Securities and Exchange Commission

 TIPS & TECHNIQUES

Because of the complexities associated with patent value, useful versus finite life, litigation risks to value, and valuation methods, the CFO should insist on meeting routinely with other engineering, legal, and IP members of the PQM Team. Together they should determine a set of baseline rules for valuing patent costs, asset value, and valuation that will be used throughout the organization. These rules, which would establish the companywide basis on which the CFO will prepare documentation and report intangible assets under FAS-142, should be reviewed routinely and compared to any emerging industry standards of practice.

(SEC) to be on heightened alert in testing the methods by which CFOs determine patent value and the depth and breadth of documentation used to support the valuation claims.

You should consider preparing certain documentation for SEC review that would at least include the following:

- Clear identification of the intellectual property
- Determination of the useful life of each patent
- Determination of whether an intangible asset has an indefinite life
- Method of valuing each patent
- Recognition of transitional impairment losses

Maximizing shareholder value under the new FAS-142 will be one of your most important overriding objectives. Embracing FAS-142 as the umbrella under which many of your PQM policies and procedures emerge will help drive a patent value mindset throughout the organization. The CEO's job now includes financial patent strategy in the purest sense. We'll see how the CFO can implement that strategy to push the tactical components of the finance department's PQM responsibilities.

Asset Creation versus Cash Generation

When looking at the plus columns of financial statements, two primary financial objectives drive patent-related decisions: (1) asset value creation, as we've discussed relative to FAS-142, and (2) cash generation.

Decisions affecting asset creation have already been discussed, and yet the ability of a patent to generate cash flow can influence its value as an asset. If a patent is projected to generate long-term cash flow as a result of licensing royalty annuities, then the earning power of the patent plays into the valuation. Historically, sales of goods and services have been considered the determiners of cash generation, yet companies are coming to understand that licensing their intellectual property can generate a disproportionately high return on assets (ROA).

In the early 1990s, IBM was earning $60 million per year from licenses to its patent portfolio. In 2001, that figure had jumped to $1.2 billion. Several authors have recently popularized the concept of capitalizing on the hidden value of patents, but brought down to a patent-by-patent level, the CFO can begin to drive incremental sales by instituting a plan to systematically license a company's patents.

In fact, Macrovision Corp. (NASDAQ: MVSN) and Dolby Laboratories, Inc. (audio technology) are just two examples of companies that rely primarily on patent licensing to generate cash. In 2000, Macrovision generated $80 million in sales from licensing its video and consumer copy protection software technology, and since developing its technology, Dolby has sold licenses for more than 950 million products, plus 60 million surround decoders and 180 million products incorporating Dolby Digital (AC-3).

In working with the marketing, engineering, and legal members of the PQM Team, the CFO can help establish a realistic balance between holding patents tightly and exploiting the technology through sales of products incorporating the protected technology, or incorporating a licensing model to separately generate cash.

Besides the obvious profit generated from licensing, it can have a much greater effect on the future of the corporation by helping make the product line the industry standard, thus reinforcing the corporation's position in a mature marketplace and its ability to survive. Of course, whenever the generation of licensing revenue becomes a business hard point, there will be an associated cost to defend the licensees from infringement. We'll discuss patent-related costs later in this chapter.

Borrowing Power

As CFOs are continuously asked to find money to fund key projects, they often turn to equity or debt financing. Mortgages, capital equipment loans, secured lines of credit, and leases are just a few of the common debt instruments that come into play when funding growth initiatives.

When it comes to making business loans, bankers are always first in line to serve you. Traditional banks and lending institutions are by nature risk adverse—a position that has served them well for centuries. But we're not talking about serving them, we're talking about serving *you*. So, if your new forms of capital have much of your tangible assets already tied up as security, and you have a solid intellectual property portfolio, you'll want to take a long look at royalty financing.

As intellectual property becomes an increasingly large part of a corporation's assets, loans based on your intellectual property (or the royalty revenue it generates) are becoming an exciting alternative to tying up equity or capital assets as loan collateral—the security with which traditional lenders are familiar. Royalty financing is a powerful tool; Disney employed royalty financing in 1992 when it borrowed $400 million against its copyright portfolio.

When you receive a loan from your traditional bank, you usually sign security agreements that ensure that the bank can access your assets if they encounter problems with loan repayment. Fair enough; however, you'll invariably find that they include a line in the security description that includes intellectual property. Your traditional bank includes that line simply because some lawyer back at the home office included it in the loan contract template they created back in 1986. The fact is that your bank probably doesn't have a clue about intellectual property, let alone what they would do with it if they ended up owning your patents or trademarks. Nevertheless, they secure it.

Traditional loans and leases that secure your IP present problems for the CFO who wants to employ an aggressive new PQM system. Besides not being able to secure new loans that leverage your patents, you can't license interest in, transfer, or otherwise manage your patents because they are pledged to the bank. The ability to manage your interest in your own intellectual property is diluted when using traditional lending mechanisms that incorporate IP as security.

More progressive lenders not only recognize the lending business opportunity, but they have become patent savvy and employ the latest

IN THE REAL WORLD

Use Patents as Loan Collateral

If you're considering using your patent royalties to secure royalty financing, here are some things to watch for:

- Review your current debt financing agreements and establish to what extent you have already secured your intellectual property against existing loans (read the fine print).

- If your IP is already used as security, either (1) negotiate with the bank to break out your intangible assets from the current collateral list, or (2) prioritize repayment of the debt so that the security is released.

- Work with other members of your company's PQM Team to identify a few key patents that could generate significant revenue from licensing income, and work these patents into the forefront of your licensing efforts. Create the maximum future royalty value because this will be the basis for determining the amount of the loan you're likely to receive.

- If you do secure royalty financing, be aware that a holdback, or reserve, may be required to cover a drop in the royalty payments based on any number of factors.

Even if you don't have current royalty streams, if you can present a plausible case to the lender, they may still consider future royalties as a loan basis. Creativity is the key. In 1997, the Bowie Bonds funded $55 million based on projected licensing revenues from rock star David Bowie's record albums, secured only by the future royalty income stream.

evaluation techniques to determine the tangible value of intangible assets, and have the wherewithal to craft unique loans based on your patent licensing royalties. One company has stepped out as an early innovator in the royalty financing space, and others are sure to follow. Royalty financing is the only loan program offered by Jericho, New York–based Licent Capital, LLC. Licent makes loans starting at $3 million using your royalty stream as the primary security.

Another company, The Pullman Group LLC, is a principal investment bank and specialty finance company servicing the entertainment and intellectual property industries. The Pullman Group is best known for creating the first-ever securitization of entertainment royalties and intellectual properties, including future music royalties for David Bowie, a $55 million transaction.

Besides being a great new source of additional funds when your tangible assets are fully encumbered, royalty financing does not dilute ownership of the intellectual property and enables the patent owner to retain all upside value of the asset. Therefore, even if your patents secure a royalty financing loan, you're still free to continue to exploit those patents via new licensing or cross-licensing agreements. For convenience, PatentCafé provides a quick-read outline of the Licent Capital loan program, as well as an online royalty finance loan application at *www.2XFR.com*.

Taxes

Taxes are always a consideration of the CFO. Where patents are concerned, several considerations may drive your tax strategy.

It's too early to understand all of the tax implications related to patents or other intangible assets since the implementation of FAS-142, so you will want to consult with your tax attorney and accountant to determine the best reporting approach for your company.

Some of the considerations in determining a patent tax strategy will include the following:

- How you will report direct and indirect costs of obtaining the patent

- How you will allocate a patent's underlying R&D costs (this will relate to how you address the impairment tests under FAS-142)

- How you may structure taxes for patents that secure loans, as well as the income or (loss) that may be realized through a license

- Litigation costs associated with defending infringement of a patent

- How you will report the acquisition of a patent portfolio, as well as the licensing revenue or litigation defense costs associated with individual properties within the portfolio

- How you may report the sale of intangible assets after you have transitioned them to the new reporting required under FAS-142

In short, patents and taxes are closely tied at many levels. Implementing a strategy that adopts a clear and consistent reporting policy under the most current IRS rulings, and that incorporates the sound advice of your tax professionals, could have a significant positive (or negative) impact on shareholder value.

Patent Budgeting

Cost of Obtaining Patents: Investing in Domestic and International Patent Protection

As you know by now, patents are incredibly valuable assets that, like other assets, can be created or improved as a result of direct investment. Although the amount of money invested in research that is hoped to

lead to an important discovery and patent is little more than a guess-
timate, the good news is that the costs related to obtaining patents are
fairly well defined.

In general, there are two financial components related to obtaining
a new patent:

1. Attorney fees in preparing the patent application, and subsequent
   patent prosecution while the patent is pending

2. Published government fees for filing the patent application, for
   communication responses with the patent office (office actions),
   for the issuance of an approved patent, and for the periodic future
   maintenance fees that are required to keep the issued patent
   active

We're not going to go into the details of attorney fees and government filing costs, but it's important for CFOs to understand the range
of costs and what the company should be receiving for its investment in
patent development.

First, CFOs should generally figure that attorney fees associated
with the preparation, filing, and prosecution of each U.S. patent will
approximate $10,000. Simple mechanical patents will be less, whereas
complicated method patents and patents related to genetic, biotechnology, chemical, and pharmaceutical inventions could go higher. Begin
obtaining quotes for each patent submitted to your attorney, and track
invoices against the quoted amount for each patent separately.

Attorney invoices will be confusing because they often incorporate
details for all of the time and expenses due for a certain period, but often
neglect to break out every matter as a separate invoice. It is common to
have many patents pending at the same time, so tracking costs associated
with any particular patent can become nearly impossible.

As a management tool to track patent costs against your budget, ask
the law firm to begin creating separate monthly invoices for activity
related to each patent. As you enter these invoice figures into your

accounting system, you will be able to track the actual costs of each patent. If you see the costs going significantly north of the amount you budgeted for any of the patents, it's time to have a meeting with the law firm.

Another benefit to this separate invoicing is your ability to report all of the directly related costs when you begin documenting intangible asset value under the FAS-142 requirements.

Second, filing, transmittal, publishing, and issuance fees for each issuing patent office will need to be budgeted for as well. In the United States, there are two fee schedules: one schedule for large entities (companies with more than 500 employees), and another schedule for small entities (companies with fewer than 500 employees). As a gauge, you can assume that all of the small entity patent office fees will generally be 50 percent of the large entity fees.

The government fees are always changing, so we're not going to pin any specific numbers on each transmittal activity; however, as a rule of thumb, companies can figure that all fees associated with the filing through issuance of a patent in the United States will be in the $3,500 to 4,000 range depending on what extras are requested, such as early

 TIPS & TECHNIQUES

Need to compare your current legal fees with what other patent attorneys are charging for similar work? Do you need a legal fee quote from a patent attorney for an unusual intellectual property–related matter? You can get some comparative budget answers quickly by entering your patent legal request for quote (RFQ) in FeeBid.com. Your RFQ will then be routed to patent attorneys nationwide, who will respond directly to you with their quotations for the work. Log in to *www.FeeBid.com.*

publication, extensions, request for hearings, and so forth. Small entities (defined by the U.S. Patent and Trademark Office as individuals and companies with fewer than 500 employees) should roughly budget half that amount, or $1,700 to $2,200.

Companies often fail to budget for patent maintenance fees because they occur years in the future. U.S. patent maintenance fees must be paid

PROPOSED 2003 PATENT OFFICE RULES

Secrets to Reduce Application Costs

New patent fees, originally scheduled to take effect in October 2002 under the new 21st Century Strategic Plan but which will likely go into effect under a modified fee legislation, are virtually guaranteed budget busters. Patent Office fees alone can reach into the tens of thousands of dollars per patent application. Compare this to the typical pre–October 2002 patent fees that run in the $3,000 to $5,000 range.

There are some advantageous strategies finance managers can take to help keep these costs down. Perhaps most important of them all would be to begin the protection process of an invention with an inexpensive provisional patent application, followed up by a regular patent application and last, requesting examination only after test marketing proves the concept to be viable and profitable. PQM Teams should not be encouraged to pursue those technologies and products that don't have a justifiable payback.

The CFO can implement project budget proposals for new product development and patent processing personnel that will take into account the effect of the new, higher fees. These budget proposals will allow the CFO to more closely control patent expenditures while working with the PQM Team to ensure that the most valuable patents receive the necessary investment support.

at intervals of 3.5 years, 7.5 years, and 11.5 years after issuance. Failure to pay these fees will result in patent abandonment. Therefore, large entities should budget about $6,000 total maintenance fee payments per patent, and small entities budget about $3,000 future maintenance fees costs for each patent.

Exhibit 8.2 summarizes the approximate budget for all preparation, filing, issuance, attorney prosecution, and maintenance fees associated with each patent filed.

Under the 21st Century Strategic Plan and October 2002 proposed fee structure, the budget would look more like Exhibit 8.3 (patent with 6 independent claims, 35 total claims, and 1 co-pending patent).

The budgeting outline so far centers on patents issued by the United States. If your company has strong overseas sales interests, international protection may be desirable. When the need for foreign patents is indicated, you will need to participate in a meeting with appropriate staff members and patent counsel to discuss the many options. On the high side, total additional patent costs to file in the many countries where you have an economic interest can easily top $100,000 per patent (some countries will have patent costs less than the United States, but others will cost more). The additional international costs will include,

---

EXHIBIT 8.2

Budget Description—Current Fee Structure

Fee Description	Large Entity	Small Entity
Attorney fees:	$10,000	$10,000*
Government filing/issue fees:	$4,000	$2,000
Patent Maintenance Fees:	$6,000	$3,000
Total Costs/New U.S. Patent:	$20,000	$15,000

*Attorney fees do not vary based on Small or Large Entity status of the applicant.

EXHIBIT 8.3

Budget Description—2003 Rules Proposed Fee Structure

Fee Description (Oct. 2002 Proposed)	Large Entity	Small Entity
Attorney fees:	$10,000	$10,000*
Government filing/issue fees:	$35,000	$17,000
Patent Maintenance Fees:	$9,000	$9,000
Total Costs/New U.S. Patent:	$54,000	$36,000

*Attorney fees do not vary based on Small or Large Entity status of the applicant.

among other things, translation services, retaining foreign patent counsel, and paying foreign filing fees. Be sure that you understand the business or economic benefit to filing patents in each country, and then budget accordingly.

 TIPS & TECHNIQUES

Filing and prosecuting patent applications in foreign countries should be considered early on because it can cost $100,000 or more depending on the countries in which you plan to file. Most countries require translation from English into their native language, which can become expensive. One international filing strategy that is used to save time and reduce cost is referred to as the checkerboard approach. In other words, file patent applications in only some countries (usually the more important ones) in a given region. Thus it makes it difficult for a potential infringer to supply only certain countries in a region and not others. This approach can be effective when foreign licensing is being considered.

Two additional patent-related costs that could be significant, and that should be budgeted for after review of the patent strategy with the technical and legal members of your team, include the following:

1. Infringement analysis and legal opinion before application filing

2. Prefiling patent value analysis—a cost/benefit analysis of the invention before filing a patent

Both of these tasks inherently incorporate a high degree of subjectivity and professional opinion; therefore, there is no actual basis for determining the fees associated with the activities. Professional or legal costs for each of these activities can range from $5,000, to more than $50,000. If either of these analyses is requested by your team, or is suggested by your patent counsel, you would do well to scrutinize the proposals and requests and determine the potential risks associated with forgoing these expenses as it may pertain to the overall budget and patent strategy.

Other costs, such as patent search, prior art search, and legal opinions regarding patentability, may pop up from time to time. They should be accounted for in the budgeting cycle, compared to the attorney fees and filing fees, but these costs combined will likely fall into the low thousands and could probably be addressed in your "other expense" line item.

 TIPS & TECHNIQUES

Finding your patents and the related technology suddenly obviated by a competitor's patents means it's time to reevaluate your company's product development activities. This kind of crisis is not necessarily bad news but is a heads-up warning that your engineering department needs to step up the R&D effort and start thinking about the next generation of products in order to get ahead—or to stay in the game.

Budget Determines Strategy

As we've seen, the direct costs of patents are significant. Filing just 10 patents in the United States and international markets annually could generate costs close to $1 million. Therefore, it's important for CFOs to include PQM initiatives in the budget planning cycle, and along with the engineering, legal, and operations staff, to establish a patent budget early each year. You should address not only the patent costs, but any licensing initiatives and corresponding royalty projections as well.

Once the budget is established, excepting extraordinary issues, the number of patent applications that engineering or legal can pursue within a given year is fairly well determined.

The CFO must also understand that technology-driven industries are dynamic and that introduction of new products by competitors, or the issuance of competitors' patents that could invalidate your pending patents, will often drive patent crisis management. Don't be afraid to

 TIPS & TECHNIQUES

Have your patent counsel conduct a general patent strategy meeting with the entire PQM Team, showing the various patent options such as filing a relatively low-cost patent cooperation treaty (PCT) application that can reserve the ability to file your application later in foreign countries. Also ask about filing multiple defensive publications, public disclosures of your technology that you can't afford to patent. Although they do not provide any ownership or protection of the technology, the public disclosure filings (costing about $100 each) will eliminate the competitor's ability to patent the technology later, which would block your company from practicing the technology in the marketplace.

suggest abandonment of patent applications if the industry changes and the potential advantage of your pending patent is all but eliminated.

The important thing to remember is that the company's budget and patent strategy go hand-in-hand, so persistently balancing patent expense against licensing revenue and protection of your technology and markets will help maximize your patent position with given resources, maximizing shareholder value.

Costs of Litigation

As CFOs know, litigation is a cost of doing business. But for litigation torts, litigation costs can be a manageable expense. Patent infringement litigation, however, can produce some extreme, business-threatening results.

There are primarily two reasons for which you may find yourself litigating your patent:

1. As a defendant in a suit that claims that your products or technology infringe another's

2. As a plaintiff claiming infringement on your intellectual property

Your patent counsel can address the legal fine points, but it's up to the CFO to assess the financial options and potential damages related to infringement litigation. Keep in mind that the median cost in the United States to bring litigation to trial during 2001 was $1.2 million. Because CFOs like to work with numbers, here are a few statistics that should factor into your initial analysis of an infringement suit:

- The average monetary award by a jury in a patent infringement case is $8.6 million.

- The average monetary award by a judge-alone in a patent infringement case is $9.8 million.

- The average loss of shareholder wealth in biotech companies when involvement in a patent suit is announced is $67.9 million.

- Patent owners have a 30 percent probability of prevailing in an infringement trial conducted in Massachusetts, but have a 68 percent probability of prevailing if the trial is held in Northern California.

If you are a defendant, having a deep patent portfolio can help drive litigation towards a cross-license settlement. Increasingly, the patent litigation world is seeing more companies that are refusing to cross-license in lieu of litigation and are simply exploiting their patents to the fullest. Some defendants are even claiming that aggressive patent enforcement borders on antitrust. If you are defending a suit brought by a plaintiff with such an aggressive history, it would be wise to convene with the PQM staff and carefully weigh the best litigation strategy.

Even before you find yourself in litigation, you may want to discuss with the PQM Team general patent strategies that should be followed throughout the organization, such as those addressed in Chapter 3.

As a plaintiff, however, the investment to initiate litigation and follow through to trial, should it progress that far, must be weighed against the potential gain. Gathering all of the important data from your team would be the starting point. This data will be necessary in constructing necessary cost/benefit analyses before proceeding with a suit, and may include the following:

- Market share being lost to the infringing company

- Actual net revenue being lost to the infringer

- The various options to the infringer to design around or their ability to quickly introduce noninfringing products as a defense to your suit (leaving you with a hollow and potentially costly victory)

- The actual strength of the patent you wish to assert (One important risk assessment would be to analyze your position if the defendant found existing prior art and actually caused your patent to be invalidated by the Patent Office.)

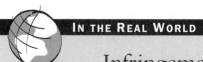

Infringement Is Costly

Most patent infringement cases are settled out of court, even if a formal complaint has been filed. Faced with the high cost of defense and invalidating a patent, a greater probability of losing, plus the significant exposure to paying a large award, infringers are usually willing to settle these issues out of court. The following chart shows that in fiscal year 2000, more than 80 percent of the infringement cases are settled without court action or before pretrial.

Significant Patent Infringement Settlements

Texas Instruments v. Hyundai	$1,000,000,000	May 99	Wall Street Journal
Texas Instruments v. Samsung	$1,000,000,000	Nov 96	Wall Street Journal
Pitney Bowes v. Hewlett Packard	$400,000,000	Jun 01	Wall Street Journal
Medtronic v. Siemens	$300,000,000	Sep 92	Wall Street Journal
Intermedics v. Cardiac Pacemakers	$250,000,000	Sep 98	National Law Journal
Gemstar v. General Instruments	$200,000,000	Nov 00	National Law Journal
University of California v. Genentech	$200,000,000	Nov 99	Press Release
Genentech v. Eli Lilly	$145,000,000	Jan 95	Wall Street Journal
P&G v. Keebler, Nabisco, Frito Lay	$125,000,000	Sep 89	New York Times
Kimberly-Clark v. Paragon Trade	$115,000,000	Mar 99	PR Newswire
Odetics v. Storage Technology	$100,000,000	Oct 99	Press Release
C.R. Bard v. Guidant	$100,000,000	Apr 98	Business Press

- Whether the infringing company was aware of the infringement because willful infringement can bring treble damage awards

Statistically, only 1.1 percent of all patents issued will become the subject of a lawsuit. While no statistics are available regarding valuable patents, you can be assured that if your PQM Team invested in patents wisely (you created valuable patents that protect a large market), the likelihood of finding yourself embroiled in a suit can be much greater. Companies don't litigate worthless patents.

It's clear that the ringing of the litigation bell can take a heavy toll on shareholders' worth, so putting some guidelines in place to address patent litigation before it happens will help not only to preserve shareholder value, but to possibly enhance it as well.

Patent Infringement Insurance

You insure everything else in your business, so why not patents? As we have just reviewed, the costs of patent litigation are extremely high, and the potential loss of shareholder worth is even higher. The vagaries of litigation push the potential exposure to financial loss even further. Patent infringement insurance has been around for some time, but as the number of infringement suits continues to rise, it is becoming a popular option for more companies that believe their patents will likely end up in suit.

There are two basic kinds of infringement insurance:

1. *Abatement insurance* which is called into play when you pursue another company infringing your patent (assertion against infringement)

2. *Infringement insurance* which, like other insurance, is invoked to help guard against casualty loss (infringement defense)

Annual infringement policy premiums are relatively affordable, especially when compared to litigation costs, and can range from $2,500 for a $250,000 infringement defense policy to a low of $1,500 for an infringement abatement policy with a $100,000 per-claim limit. You can purchase policies with limits as high as $5 million per claim.

Before issuing an infringement policy, the underwriter will perform his or her own due diligence and patent value analysis to determine the premium and policy limit amounts. Like medical insurance, they will insure patents currently caught up in litigation, but they would consider the current litigation as a preexisting condition and exclude the current case from the policy coverage.

Several insurance companies entered the infringement insurance arena over the past few years, including Chubb, Lloyds of London, AIG, The Hartford Group, and others, so there are plenty of policies to review. The more progressive insurance brokers will often offer infringement insurance, but infringement insurance specialists with a strong background in intellectual property will often be able to better guide you through the various options. Infringement insurance carriers also offer many premium add-on options that can be tailored to your single patent or the entire portfolio.

Obtaining a premium quotation is as easy as filling out an insurance request form online. PatentCafé provides an overview of various infringement insurance programs, as well as an online quotation request form, at *www.2XFR.com.*

As you work with other staff members in developing the PQM plan, at least for your most valuable patents, infringement insurance could prove to be another powerful, yet affordable tool in your arsenal.

Cost of IPAM Software

The first obvious difference between IP management systems and the engineering, accounting, and manufacturing management systems already in place in your organization is that while computer-assisted drafting (CAD), just-in-time (JIT), and other systems are *savings justified* (i.e., intended to increase efficiency, boost profits, and cut costs), intellectual property asset management (IPAM) tools are additionally positioned as *revenue generators.*

IPAM tools will squeeze efficiency out of bloated operations, but they also provide the ability of helping generate sales early in the technology development cycle, expand market share through strategic market analysis/competitive IP analysis, and through long-term royalty generation that may continue even after the normal product lifecycle. Consequently, implementing appropriate IP tools will become a competitive necessity—not an efficiency luxury.

IPAM software is increasingly being used to help manage intellectual property—from patent data mining to analysis to fees maintenance. For years, small IPAM programs have helped attorneys maintain their intellectual property docket calendars, track royalty payments, and maintain patent maintenance fee payment schedules.

Over the past three to four years, along with the advent of the Internet, more IPAM systems have emerged, promising more sophisticated patent work flow management, patent value analysis, electronic filing of patent applications, competitive analysis software that tracks a competitor's marketing or business activity by referencing its patents, and patent database search tools.

We're not going to spend a lot of time describing the functional differences between all of these systems, but we will split them into two major groups (just as you may have done when you first examined integrated accounting systems).

Discrete Function IPAM Tools. These software tools have been designed for specific purposes and with a specific user in mind. As the title suggests, these tools were developed to operate independent of any integrated system, and in most cases, are used to perform a single task. Examples of discrete function tools include (1) *docket management sys-*

tems; typical user: patent attorney/corporate counsel, (2) *patent roy-alty/annuity payment management systems;* typical user: accounting department/intellectual property consulting services firm, and (3) *patent analysis/patent mapping system;* typical user: corporate IP researcher.

These tools can be either standalone software programs or Web-based applications. Prices for these tools when purchased as software to be installed on the user's computer range from $500 to $15,000. When available as Web-based software, they are usually sold as monthly subscriptions ranging from $29 per month for each user to $15,000 per month per installation. By comparison, between 1998 and 2001, several companies offered patent analysis systems that cost upward of $100,000. More flexible and affordable systems will continue to appear on the market, so care must be made in assessing the software options.

If you could look back to the earliest accounting tools, you would see the chaos that would have occurred if payroll had its discrete function software, sales had its standalone order management system, and manufacturing had its own inventory management system. IPAMs are going through that genesis now, so your expertise in looking at cross-department functionality will come into play.

Integrated Functionality IPAM Tools. New IPAM tools are emerging that integrate many of these discrete patent management functions into a complete integrated solution, not unlike the evolution of integrated accounting systems. The system comprises modules specifically tailored to each functional operation within an organization, yet all of the activity is integrated into a central system.

For instance, a patent search module that accesses a patent database can be used by the engineering or legal department. By using this same patent database as a core, marketing can perform patent modeling of a competitor to visualize technology trends being pursued, possibly indicating their next logical product technology; however, while the legal department is more interested in patent prior art, the marketing department would have little interest in reading patent claims. A prime example of a patent database core IPAM is *http://ERP.patentcafe.com.*

Integrated IPAM tools, comparable to integrated accounting systems that begin with the General Ledger core, can be built or upgraded one module at a time, so they are now very affordable, can grow with your corporate needs, and are indispensable. If your budget won't allow for the purchase of an entire system at the start, you may be able to capitulate to the engineering department's request for a system, as long as it is the engineering module of an integrated IPAM system upon which you can add the marketing department's module at a later date.

You should run through this checklist before authorizing any single user or department budget request for IPAM software tools:

1. What will this tool do to save time or money (quantify it)?

2. How will this tool enhance your competitive intelligence?

3. Is training required before the user becomes proficient? How much training is required, and what is the cost?

4. What functional departments can use this tool, and how? (e.g., Engineering is requesting this software, can the marketing department also use it for marketing?)

5. Will this tool help create shareholder value (your determination)?

6. Is it cost justified (the answer should be "yes" if the IPAM is properly implemented within your organization)?

Your IT department manager will invariably have his or her own checklist, such as required computer platform, software security, and other technical issues, and working together with your CIO/CTO, you will be able to develop a reasonable budget that can help ensure that the proper IPAM tools can ultimately be deployed companywide.

Each of the IPAM systems considered should be tested against the company's functional requirements before considering any cost/benefit you may realize if they are implemented.

Valuation
Art and Science

Authors and analysts claiming to know how to pin a value on intellectual property fill the shelves, and it seems as if nearly as many white papers have been written about intellectual property valuation techniques as the number of issued patents. The reality is that no single formula or analysis tool can establish an objective value on any piece of intellectual property. The best IP valuation tools incorporate a high degree of computer modeling but thereafter require a certain degree of subjective human analysis. At worst, valuation is established simply by drawing artistic conclusions such as: "Company A just licensed its patent for $10 million, so our patent for a similar technology must be worth as much."

Eye of the Beholder Portfolio and Asset Acquisitions

Actions and investment decisions in a capitalistic environment all must point to economic growth and profits, so it stands to reason that in an effort to quantify a patent, the focus quickly points toward valuation. One of the reasons why it is so difficult to establish an absolute value of a patent is because everyone doing so will have his or her own desired outcome, and the valuation methods used will be selected to bias the value in support of the evaluator's objectives. For example, a company acquiring a patent portfolio from a smaller, economically disadvantaged company will want to use a valuation method that will devalue the portfolio as much as possible, so a smaller price is paid. Conversely, when the acquiring company elects to license some of the acquired technology, it will opt for a valuation method that maximizes the value.

Aside from the nuances of posturing and negotiating the acquisition, license, or sale of intellectual property, there is another objective:

Develop a valuation method that will withstand shareholder, SEC, and IRS scrutiny, as well as audits conducted on your FAS-142 documentation.

Now, we have the buyer's, seller's, and auditor's objectives that drive the choice of valuation methodology. If each of the valuation methods actually produces different results, and it will, then how does one develop an objective value? One doesn't. The fact that selection of the methodology is subjective dispels any argument that one method is more objective, or accurate, than another.

Establishing Patent Fair Market Value

Several methodologies are used to establish fair market value. We will walk though those methods here, but we will stop short of drilling into the underlying theories, algorithms, or computer and financial models.

If you will be charged with determining patent or intellectual property portfolio valuation, we encourage you to read *Essentials of Intellectual Property* by Paul J. Lerner and Alexander I. Poltorak (New York: John Wiley & Sons, 2002), which does an excellent job of explaining the most current IP valuation methods, tools, and formulae, and the appropriate application of each.

In licensing, the following three major models can help the parties reach an agreeable strike price.

Quantitative: Economic Modeling (Fairness: Good; Accuracy: Fair). There are several readily available tools, accessible via the Internet, that determine patent value based on a set of economic metrics.

One method, the TRRU Metrics method offered through PLX Systems, Inc. *(www.pl-x.com)* attempts to apply the Black–Scholes model for options pricing to industry technology segments. This method biases the result, however, because in part, there is insufficient patent licensing volume to establish reliable volatility models.

Another computer modeling approach offered by PatentRatings.com incorporates a numerical ranking, or score, based on several patent metrics determined to have a statistically significant relationship to observed patent maintenance rates. This model ignores actual industry or economic performance but deduces industry performance by assuming that high-value patents in any segment would not be abandoned; therefore, the patent maintenance fees would be paid. The cost per patent analysis is about $125.00.

PatentValuePredictor, yet another on-demand computer analysis tool, calculates the value of a given patent based on several economic factors, including the relative percentage of the gross domestic product (GDP), the remaining life of the patent, the industry segment, and other factors. PatentValuePredictor is one of the valuation tools offered by PatentCafé through *www.2XFR.com*. Cost per patent analysis is about $100.

Keep in mind that forward-looking valuation, regardless of the method used, is not absolute, so determining an actual value quantitatively is extremely difficult. The methodology offered through these computer modeling tools is, in part, used by patent valuation services, which add a human (subjective) element to the formula.

Qualitative: Comparable Deals (Fairness: Very Good; Accuracy: Good). By reviewing recent licensing agreements executed by other companies within your industry or technology segment, you can begin to paint a picture of the going-market value of similar technologies. Although other deals are a good reference point, they do not accurately reflect the nuances that differ in every deal.

Cost Method: Budget Driven (Fairness: Very Poor; Accuracy: Very Good). This method is accurate from the licensee's point of view because it reflects precisely the amount of money a licensee has budgeted to acquire a technology; however, this method disregards the needs or objectives of the inventor/technology owner. In essence, it lays out the framework for an adversarial take it or leave it negotiation.

A second adversarial approach to value determination positions a defendant in an infringement litigation as a potential licensee, but only if the defendant has established its litigation budget and decided that licensing is the more economical approach. If a plaintiff pushes for too high a value, the infringer may resort to extreme measures in an attempt to either invalidate the asserted patent or devalue the plaintiff's position, leaving the prospective licensor without financial gain.

Financial Roll-Up

As the financial hub of an organization, the CFO shoulders the burden of budgeting and managing financial performance for the benefit of the shareholders. As the financial hub of the PQM Team, the CFO drives and monitors patent value performance. Because intellectual property management has found itself in the business spotlight, the importance of managing the many elements of intellectual property creation, maintenance, exploitation, and value enhancement have become performance milestones for gauging overall financial performance. With the tools outlined in this chapter, the CFO becomes an important member of the PQM Team, helping to create and maintain an organization's intellectual property growth and vitality.

CHAPTER 9

Managing Patents in the Human Resources Department

After reading this chapter you will be able to

- Understand the relationship of patent management to the human resources department—human capital is the source of intellectual property

- Learn how to develop, implement, and manage a Patent Quality Management Team

- Understand the importance of training to foster an awareness of striving for superior processes and innovations

- Learn how to track, monitor, and reward an employee's contribution to the company's patent development

C ross-functional organizations consist of department heads, section managers, and senior staff, all working to leverage the value of the company's technology and patents. The larger the organization, the more difficult it is to communicate across all of the functional areas.

Organizations also employ people—the human capital that the company relies on to create value in its intellectual property. Thus it is important that the company receive the full benefit of the employee–employer relationship, whether the employee works in engineering, marketing, manufacturing, or in any other company department.

So, while Human Resources (HR) may appear to have little or nothing to do with patents, the fact is that HR is often the company's communication and training hub, as well as the keeper of employee records and documentation—all critical components to an effective Patent Quality Management system.

IN THE REAL WORLD

HR Managers Are Responsible for Patents, Too

Agreements between the company and employee can often keep financially damaging events from occurring. Other times, employees who join a competitive company become the center of negative attention, as in the suit between Intel and Broadcom.

In March 2000, the Santa Clara County Superior Court issued a preliminary injunction preventing Broadcom from disclosing, using or acquiring Intel trade secrets.

Broadcom shares opened at $250.38 that day and climbed as high as $257. But as investors received word of the suit, which was reported first by CNET News.com, the shares began to slide. In late trading, the shares dipped to as low as $232.75 before closing at $238.44.*

Intel previously filed a complaint against Broadcom in California Superior Court in Santa Clara. That complaint, filed on March 8, 2000, alleged misappropriation of Intel trade secrets. It was based on Broadcom's hiring of Intel employees. The Court issued a Preliminary Injunction against Broadcom on May 25, 2000.

The question is, if HR had worked with the IP management team, corporate counsel, and IP counsel, would more effective IP-related employee agreements have been in place that could have salvaged Broadcom's legal position (and shareholder value)?

*Source: *Tech Law Journal.*

Responsibilities: Implement and Manage Capturing All Corporate Innovation

We know that engineers put their thoughts on paper, their designs on CAD systems, and their inventions in their engineering journals. Similarly, marketing managers scribble their new product ideas on napkins during lunch and develop sales projections and competitive analysis charts on spreadsheets. Manufacturing experts are always trying to figure out new ways to make production run faster, smoother, with less downtime and fewer defects.

So it would seem that engineering, marketing, manufacturing, and other operational groups within an organization all inherently have a method of capturing an employee's inventive work product; however, without a central information management hub, there is little correlation between what information the company captures from computers and napkin creations and long-term patent portfolio value. All of this intellectual property, the essential work product of a company's employees, represents an incredible investment by the company, an investment that must produce tangible results.

So, when we assemble the company's collective knowledge (intellectual capital), the obligation to harvest and manage that intellectual capital for the benefit of the shareholders, and determine the management mechanisms needed to nurture, contain, and grow intellectual property and patent portfolios, all fingers expectedly point to Human Resources.

The Human Resources department brackets an employee's time with the company. It is the department that recruits and hires, as well as hands out pink slips, accepts resignations, and coordinates retirements. It is the first and last point of contact an employee will have with an employer, so no department head has more control over what information comes into the company, what information escapes, and what information remains as equitable work product by all employees than the HR manager.

Policy Development

The HR manager has an extraordinarily strong voice among the PQM Team when it comes to corporate IP policy development. After all, policies all trickle down to day-to-day employee practices, including employee new-hire packets, training, coaching, monitoring, performance reviews, prehire screening, and exit interviews.

In turn, HR must depend heavily on finance, legal, and other key PQM members because local and state labor laws, special work conditions, corporate insurance programs, and so forth all affect the final version of an employee policy. HR must start planning long before installing the PQM system in order to play its part in implementation. More specifically, planning must be done in the areas of policy development, employee training, employee records management practices, employee recognition programs, and gathering a collection of IP-related forms and agreements applicable to all temporary or permanent employees.

Implementing the Policy

Communicating company mission statements or business charters throughout an organization is nearly impossible, even though these are the company essentials. So is it going to be any easier communicating a company's patent management or intellectual property policy right down to the production worker? Probably not.

HR is usually expert in communicating programs throughout an organization, so program implementation, or at least communication, of the PQM system will fall most often to the HR department. There will typically be a large number of changes companywide, and in older organizations many people who traditionally resist change.

Managing the Structure: Continuous Training

As in total quality management (TQM), patent quality management is a continuous process of improvement. Improvement in a PQM system sometimes takes on an unfamiliar definition such as "reduced litigation costs," "increased manufacturing process inventions," or "increased intangible asset value." Most employees will simply not have a clue as to what these terms mean, let alone contribute to their improvement.

HR has traditionally been the center of corporate training when important new practices and policies are enacted companywide. Patent quality management and shareholder value enhancement through patent management will be entirely new concepts to most employees, even to most engineers. Continuous training programs will be a critical component of your PQM system. In working with the other key staff (engineering, manufacturing, finance, and other cross-functional executives), HR must build a training program that all executives wholeheartedly buy into and support. The implementation should be scheduled so that all employees learn about, embrace, then contribute to patent quality management companywide.

Employee Hiring Practices

HR also has a unique responsibility, or perhaps better said, a unique *opportunity* in the new employees it seeks out and hires. Nobody understands the various unique personality styles better than an HR manager. So the question arises: Does the present employee mix have the creative people it needs? Or, is the present mix a team of people that does nothing more, or nothing less, than what they are told to do?

Seeking out, screening, and evaluating new hires takes on a new definition within a PQM system. As an HR manager, you know the fundamentals you seek in an employee, but have you also considered how these employees may impact the IP portfolio of the company? Are you aware of the various personality styles that tend to contribute toward creative, problem-solving efforts?

The three departments that must have the right blend of personnel or the right kind of employees are manufacturing, marketing, and engineering. Finding the right employee personality styles depends on your company's present market position and its future intentions. An employee mismatch can have disastrous effects on new inventive product developments and marketing efforts.

Manufacturing Personnel

Older, more well-established companies tend to have, and to hire, manufacturing employees who won't rock the boat. This may be okay for high-volume, generic production, but it may present problems when developing new, inventive product lines. One reason that the senior employees won't rock the boat is that it is inherent in their personality style. That's why they've been there so long anyway.

A common attitude in large, immovable departments is CYA. Of course we know this attitude translates to "don't try anything new," which begs the question, "How can anything inventive take place in a plant if employees are afraid to contribute?"

New, innovative products often require new, innovative manufacturing processes and techniques. Experience helps, but thinking outside the box helps even more. This is one of the qualities that creative, innovative personnel can bring that CYA employees can't. Besides, established employees often believe that new products taken on by the corporation will take sales away from existing product lines and will result in employee layoffs. The very survival of the company may depend on the development of the new product line. Manufacturing people of a new product line within your company have to know how to jump through hoops to get the invention launched.

If your company is a new, innovative one, you're probably already using the most up-to-date personality scan and test methods. On the other hand, if your company is an older, more well-established one, regardless of whether you are embarking in a new direction, don't be afraid to attack the status quo and seek out those new employees that can provide creative solutions to old problems or contribute to your new endeavor.

The success of your PQM system is directly related to your manufacturing department's ability to turn out a high volume of high-quality, patented products. That is what management and shareholders are depending on. Focusing your hiring practice on those individuals who can spearhead and support this effort is tantamount to success.

 IN THE REAL WORLD

Think Out of the Box . . . er, Bag

In the early 1990s, most of the paper grocery sack companies went out of business and were replaced by plastic grocery sack companies instead. One reason the paper companies could not respond to the challenge was because of their paper bag manufacturing mentality. The plastic sack manufacturing process was different. It was a fast, flexible manufacturing process and required new skills to address new challenges and solve new problems. Almost every paper bag company that attempted to go into the plastic grocery sack business either failed or sold out as a result. This included Princeton (St. Regis), Cupples, Zellerbach, Longview, and Willamette Industries. On the other hand, Trinity did the smart thing and opened an entirely separate plastic bag manufacturing facility and is thriving today.

Sales/Marketing Personnel

Many good ideas have gone astray because a company's marketing team does not want to, or cannot, sell a new innovation. Believe it or not, this happened to IBM with the invention of the PC. Its sales team was dedicated to large supercomputers and had no interest in taking on cheap ones. As reported about the salespeople, "They'd simply have to sell too much to make the same commissions."

Generally speaking, there are two different types of sales/marketing people. One is very good at order-taking, maintaining current market share, and keeping present customers happy. The other type is much more entrepreneurial. They get great pleasure in launching new products and concepts and creating markets. They are also quick to evaluate and identify new inventive attributes and make suggestions on what needs to change in order to be successful. These kinds of marketing individuals tend to be harder to find, but are invaluable in new inventive efforts.

When evaluating new hires for employment in the sales/marketing department, the innovation-oriented company must look for these kinds of individuals. You know who they are—they have many past recent successes in launching new products. They tend to be more enthusiastic about their work, intent on problem solving, and perceptive of true customer needs.

There is one other consideration with new hires in the marketing department. Customer service support personnel must be those kinds of individuals who also know how to solve problems and make things happen. They have to have great communication skills and be able to get to the bottom of any problem. Launching new products requires a highly responsive support team.

All told, your PQM system must have aggressive, market creation–type sales personnel and supporting cast. Nothing happens until something gets sold, and order takers won't get you there.

Engineering Personnel

We know that one of the keys to the future success of any company is the ability to engineer and design new patented products and improvements. This responsibility is primarily that of the engineering department. Did you know that most engineers are taught principles that deal with well-known subject matter? Whether that is stress, force, electrical, conductive, or chemical properties, it basically deals with established norms. But invention deals with the unknown. After all, it wouldn't be patentable if it were already in the public domain. Newly discovered inventive principles are often contrary to already known subject matter.

What does this mean when hiring engineers? It means that inventive, PQM-oriented companies have to find those engineers who challenge existing norms, those who have versatile minds that can consider all the relative phenomena that contribute to a new invention. They must be able to think in terms of complex associations and combinations in order to get the desired effects.

The creative engineer flourishes in the PQM environment. Your challenge is to find those engineers who want to challenge today's norms, who want to solve problems and create new concepts, those who understand who is the real customer. When these people are pointed in the right direction and set free, they often become a powerful patent mill.

Training

We know that training pervades every aspect of every department in the corporation, but even though patents and intellectual property may represent a high percentage of the corporation's asset value, there is very little, if any, training for PQM.

Human Resources has a tremendous opportunity to change that: To teach an awareness and the importance of striving for superior manufacturing processes, more highly desirable, customer-driven innovations, and sales that are protected by patents.

Top-Down Policy Facilitators

Leadership training has long followed the principle of leading by example. If senior staff fails to buy into a companywide policy such as PQM, one cannot expect middle-level managers or employees to follow the program.

HR managers should have learned long ago that any company policy training program must start at the top—in the corner office, with the CEO. We'll be frank: If the CEO fails to buy into your patent and invention education and training programs, then you really do not have such a program. Patent management requires personnel, commitment, budget, and program implementation, none of which will occur without the CEO's endorsement.

Once the training objectives are established by the team, HR can then develop the materials and begin scheduling training seminars throughout the year. Begin with the senior staff, then down to middle management, and last to lower-level employees. Let it become known throughout the company that all the VPs are taking patent management training and that the new patent management system represents great potential for job security. The HR department must communicate the specifics that are relevant to each particular department and how that department's role represents an important part of the overall company's team effort.

For those companies that have successfully introduced a Quality Management system, the PQM model is similar—only a lot easier and a lot more fun, too. But the benefits of a PQM system may actually have a greater impact in today's business world with the high value placed on patents and intellectual property rights.

Introducing PQM

The introduction begins by announcing to every employee that a new PQM system is being introduced, that every employee shall be a part of the new system, and that it is a permanent system. This is best accomplished by issuing a friendly letter discussing the new PQM system and its importance, and including other pertinent forms, such as patent assignment agreements.

The letter of introduction communicates the following:

- The importance of PQM includes protecting company assets, developing new inventive products and improvements, and ensuring long-term job security.

- All employees must participate in order to have continuity and develop cross-departmental teams.

- All manufacturing operations are considered trade secrets and shall remain confidential, regardless of how simple and basic they may seem.

- Each employee shall have an opportunity to contribute to new, inventive concepts, and that too shall remain confidential.

- PQM management teams and development teams will be appointed.

- All employees are made aware that any new discovery they make will be assigned to the company.

- Employees are asked to acknowledge (sign) the letter and assignment agreement.

This is your company's first step toward managing its confidential information, protecting its patent assets, and setting the course for a prosperous future.

Employee Files

Every company uses employee W-4 forms, the Federal I-9 form, 401 election forms, health insurance signup forms, and a resume and employment application, but they should make sure that every employee file also contains a comprehensive intellectual property section. It has always been considered a part of engineering employee files, but intellectual property and invention can originate from anywhere within the company. The concept of engineers being the heart and soul of corporate patent development is a thing of the past. So too are the traditional notions that only engineers create inventions.

Today, the HR manager must take a serious look at *all employees* across all departments. Opportunities abound to protect internal processes and systems that contribute to the longevity of the company—whether manufacturing, safety, training, or marketing related. With added importance on inventing and creating new products that are customer driven, marketing personnel are in a position to identify and contribute more than other departments. Besides, they are usually more sensitive to real customer needs than engineering.

Invention Assignments

In the United States, patents can only be issued to individuals—inventors. In order for the rights in the patent to be transferred from an inventor to the company, the inventor must execute an invention assignment agreement.

Traditionally, companies required only technical employees to sign invention assignment agreements at the start of their employment; however, as we've seen throughout this book, almost anyone in the company could ultimately become a named inventor on important company patents, whether technically trained or not. Therefore, it will be increasingly important for HR to implement companywide employment policies that routinely include invention assignment agreements.

The invention assignment agreements used throughout the company will probably vary depending on the management level (higher-level access to confidential information) and the technical skill level of the employee.

There are basically three patent management forms that HR should use in conjunction with employee files:

1. *Invention Assignment and Confidentiality Agreement.* The mechanism that transfers rights of intellectual property created by the employee for the company's benefit.

2. *List of Inventions.* A comprehensive listing of all inventions made by the employee before joining your company.

3. *Termination Certifications.* A supplemental agreement executed by the employee upon employment termination in which employees certify they have delivered to the company all intellectual property and patent records, and that they have no confidential or proprietary company information in their possession.

You should not use legal agreements or forms unless and until your corporate counsel has given final approval on the form and content of the agreement. The forms discussed in this book are not a substitute for proper legal counsel and are only intended to familiarize HR managers with terms and terminology that would be encountered in patent- and invention-related agreements used with employees.

Policies for Engineers

Most engineers understand the importance of maintaining daily logs and a paper trail of drawings, improvements, and at times, prototypes. Specifically for engineers, they should be completing the following tasks:

- Daily logs and records must be clear, concise, properly dated, and an individual who understands the inventive matter must sign the pages to verify the content.

- Drawings should be archived, regardless of whether they have been improved on at a later date. If inventorship is ever challenged in court, there may be no better way to illustrate the first, true inventor than by producing a series of drawings that show the metamorphosis of the concept.

● Verify and prove all new engineering concepts with all departments they affect. Your company must maintain its customer-driven innovation approach and cannot chance turning into an archaic manufacturing-driven company.

● Set sights on innovating for the end user customer and working with marketing to develop and validate these new concepts.

Once the new policy is in place, it may represent new challenges and a new direction for the company's engineers. But this is how it should be—must be—in order to ensure the company's future prosperity.

Policies for Technical Personnel

Technicians may be in manufacturing or R&D-related operations. Or in larger corporations, they may be in any sideways division such as safety or maintenance.

Surprisingly, there is great opportunity to discover new inventive matter through the efforts of these individuals. After all, they are the ones who work hands-on producing existing products and processes, and at times proving and developing new ones. Your technicians could be the company's front line toward identifying new patentable concepts, especially new processes that will literally make their job easier. Sometimes, you only need to ask.

For those keen individuals who have identified a new concept worthy of development, you will want to introduce them to the daily log system and methodology. They will become an important part of the PQM development team to evaluate and implement the concept should it prove to be valuable.

Manufacturing technicians and personnel must also be clearly advised that all manufacturing trade secrets and operating data are strictly confidential and that they may never be used or revealed to others should the employee choose to leave the company or be terminated for whatever reason. This is usually the function of the introductory letter, but it should also be acknowledged separately in writing.

Policies for Managers

Managers' PQM policies are two-fold. First, almost all managers have a great opportunity to contribute to the patent portfolio because experience plays an important part in identifying and developing new opportunities and concepts. Thus they too may use daily logs and will participate in PQM development teams as well.

But perhaps a more important role is that of being a facilitator within the department. Good management means acknowledging others and their good ideas. No employee can be discouraged from submitting or discussing a new inventive concept. There must be a free flow of information in order to encourage a team effort; it's the manager's responsibility to encourage it.

Employee Recognition

Employee recognition remains one of the proven, most effective ways to reinforce a company's culture, retain top talent, and support overall corporate objectives. In a recent poll of employees in Fortune 500 companies, only 46 percent of the employees said "My manager provides ample and effective recognition." In other words, more than half of the employees felt that the company did not adequately recognize their achievements or contributions to the organization.

Recognition for sales employees has been rooted in corporate tradition for decades. As company emphasis shifts from manufacturing assets, to sales and revenue numbers, to building value through intangible assets, so too must the metrics for employee recognition change.

It is important to not confuse employee *recognition* with employee *reward*. Rewards such as a commission bonus or a company-paid weekend vacation are usually tied to events or milestone achievements (such as hitting sales targets for the month or opening the new store ahead of schedule). Recognition, on the other hand, is not event driven, but rather process driven. It promotes more of a long-term spirit of achievement within the corporate environment.

Recognizing an employee for issuing a patent raises new issues for the HR manager. First, patent issuance is an event similar to hitting a sales target, yet there should not necessarily be a financial reward tied directly to the patent. Second, splitting patent recipients from the employee population without also recognizing other employees who have contributed to innovation and invention that may not have resulted in a patent can actually unwind the employee cohesiveness you're trying to build in the first place. So, when it comes to employee recognition programs that celebrate contributions to invention and company intellectual property, HR is tasked with creating its own innovative program. Clearly, this book is not intended to be a manual for Human Resources. You probably already have an employee recognition program of one kind or another, so there is no need to cover old ground.

The first step in structuring an employee recognition program to address achievement in patents, invention, and innovation is to meet with the PQM Team and develop achievement metrics, budgets, the scope of the recognition program, and the program goals. With the HR manager as the program sponsor, recognition team members should then consist of cross-functional employees who can objectively assess contributions to innovation and invention (not just engineer's patents) that should be considered for recognition.

An effective recognition program will not necessarily wait for an event ending before the celebration begins. Although a patent issuance signifies an end event, patents are issued years after the employee creates the invention, and often, after the employee leaves the company. Therefore, it is important to recognize employees who are making demonstrable advances toward innovation and invention development, portfolio value enhancement, or commercial patent exploitation.

Named Inventor versus Team Recognition

Another problem with inventor recognition programs is the difficulty in recognizing the inventor employee who may have received a patent, while similarly recognizing the other noninventor team members who assisted in creating the prototype, conducting background research, or otherwise contributed significantly to the invention. Not only is the team morale at stake, but in the spirit of the PQM system, it's the team

TIPS & TECHNIQUES

Conduct Employee Recognition Surveys

Communication and feedback are critical to developing and managing an effective patent and innovation recognition program. Given the new objectives of increasing shareholder value through effective patent development, management, and exploitation, it is important that all employees who will participate in the PQM system believe that they are being adequately recognized for their valuable contributions. Asking employees what they want in their recognition program is one of the most important things HR can do when creating a new innovation recognition program.

Companywide, implement 24/7 access for employees to provide feedback on the employee recognition program, either by e-mail, internal phone number, or feedback form on the company's Website.

that builds patent-related value throughout an organization, not only the patent recipient.

Remember also that the corporate goal of a PQM system is to increase overall shareholder value. Not only do patents on new inventions contribute to shareholder value, but when the finance team successfully acquires a patent portfolio, or when the legal team successfully defends a patent infringement suit, shareholders also benefit. Building an employee recognition program around patent issuance obviously disregards the contributions made by other noninventor employees.

Although an inventor may be recognized as the patent recipient during an annual employee recognition event, make sure that the recognition is a component of recognizing each individual on the team, and the team as a whole with regards to meeting the goals of increasing shareholder value.

Financial Awards

Employees are hired to do a job. If that job is in the technical field, the work product could ultimately result in a patent. Technical employees are, by job description, being paid to create inventions and patents. Paying financial awards to employees who receive patents can set a precedent that will make corporatewide expansion of the PQM plan

 TIPS & TECHNIQUES

To find inventor awards for your recognition awards event, search Google.com for **"corporate inventor recognition."** These companies also supply corporate lobby and "wall of fame" inventor recognition centers for businesses.

expensive and inequitable (noninventors will never receive a patent, and thus will never receive a patent award).

Although employees have already executed invention assignment agreements, there is no need to purchase or license rights to the patent from the employee. Nevertheless, some companies have adopted a payment to the inventor/employee as official recognition of the transfer of patent rights. In some companies, this amount is a token one dollar ($1.00), whereas other companies have established a financial award of $1,000 per patent issued. These numbers are not big, but they do recognize the inventor with a fixed price financial award, as opposed to setting up a system that creates subjective compensation amounts or financial awards tied to sales of the invention.

So how much financial award should be budgeted? We think you will find that a budget of $100 per year per employee is more than adequate to recognize and award all inventor and noninventor employees who have contributed to the patent and intellectual property value enhancement during the year.

Companies that Recognize Inventors in the Hall of Fame

Increasingly, companies of every size are taking a more assertive approach to recognizing inventors and contributors to corporate innovation. Although the company examples that follow are commendable, they seem to focus more on inventors rather than the PQM team members. Nevertheless, these examples provide a glimpse into the employee invention recognition programs and can well serve as a model for a broader invention and innovation recognition program.

Illinois Tool Works (NYSE: ITW). In 2001, Illinois Tool Works had more than 17,000 patents and pending patent applications worldwide, including 3,000 U.S. patents and 1,200 pending U.S. applications.

Illinois Tool Works routinely ranks in the top 100 list of U.S. patent recipients.

In 1969, Illinois Tool Works founded the ITW Patent Society to celebrate, institutionalize, and reward commercial innovations and success. During its annual dinner awards ceremony, the company recognizes the patent contributions of its product design and engineering people. Since its founding, more than 562 employees have been inducted into the Patent Society, including employees ranging from the CEO to engineers, to salespeople. Even within the Patent Society, the company tries to recognize the superachievers, with more than 130 of the members having been recognized as Distinguished Fellows for having patents on inventions for products of noteworthy commercial success.

Delphi Automotive Systems (NYSE: DPH). Delphi Automotive Systems posts some incredible innovation numbers itself. In 2000, Delphi received 597 patents worldwide (more than two patents each working day), and its engineers submitted more than 2,400 invention disclosures (about 10 inventions each working day). But at Delphi, it's not just the numbers that count—it's the people. Every two years, Delphi inducts its most talented inventors into the company's prestigious Innovation Hall of Fame during a gala ceremony. Induction into the hall is Delphi Automotive Systems' highest technical honor. Delphi's Innovation Hall of Fame, founded in 1995, boasts more than 370 members, yet this is a small fraction of Delphi's more than 16,000 engineers, scientists, and technicians.

In addition to the honor of gaining a place in the Innovation Hall of Fame, inductees receive a marble obelisk, the Egyptian symbol of power, and their names and pictures are featured on a silver wall plaque that is displayed year-round at Delphi's World Headquarters and Customer Center in Troy, Michigan.

So while it's clear that the act of inventing happens in almost every department *except* HR, human resources must take the lead responsibility in developing employee policies that capture, for the benefit of the corporation and shareholders, all intellectual capital contributions made by employees. HR is also the hub of employee training, as well as employee recognition, both of which are critically important components of a corporate Patent Quality Management program.

CHAPTER 10

Managing Patents in the Information Technology Department

After reading this chapter you will be able to

- Learn the role of patent management in the information systems department

- Understand the basics of an intellectual property and asset management (IPAM) system

- Understand the breadth and influence of software patents in every department within the organization—manufacturing, marketing, finance, IT, and even shipping, receiving, and warehousing

- Learn to take advantage of a corporate technology exchange

Why should the CTO or IT manager care about patents? After all, isn't it the IT department's job to simply keep the company's accounting systems and communication networks running and keep hackers out of the network? More important, what patent-related contribution can the IT manager possibly make to increasing shareholder value, anyway? More than first glimpse would suggest. The functional titles that will be worn by the new generation of IT manager will include *protector* of the organization's digital and intellectual property, and *creator* of new intellectual property. In fact, smart IT managers will soon find themselves being called on to select, install, and maintain an emerging new breed of software: intellectual property and asset management solutions, or IPAMs.

In addition to managing the systems that will keep track of and maintain the company's intellectual property (an offensive posture), the IT manager will increasingly assume the role of software watchdog, managing patent-related issues related to in-house software programs, Web sites, and routines written by company employees.

Today, just about every enterprise organization has its own way of building and maintaining the IT infrastructure, so we're not going to suggest *how* to integrate any IPAM system or software development program. We will, however, provide a bird's-eye view of the growing legal, technical, and management issues you're going to find yourself increasingly addressing. With proper planning with the rest of your PQM Team, you will understand just how much corporate patent management depends on you getting up to speed.

Intellectual Property and Asset Management (IPAM) Systems
Types of IPAM Systems

What is an IPAM system? As the acronym would suggest, it is an enterprise-level software solution for managing intellectual property. That's hardly a technical definition, however. The fact is, IPAM systems are in their early adolescent phase of development and are experiencing the same trying metamorphosis period that integrated accounting systems went through a quarter of a century ago. An integrated accounting system could mean anything from time-shared access to your centralized database stored on a third-party mainframe to small, fairly customized accounting applications that would allow the accounting department to tie issued invoices to purchase orders and accounts receivable history. In short, integrated accounting was anything but fully integrated.

It's also interesting to recall that integrated accounting systems were introduced for the accounting department. There was no perceived need for accounting in the marketing or IT departments, yet as the accounting system matured, the IT group managed it, the marketing group entered sales orders into it, then manufacturing confirmed shipment, and accounting billed the customer—finally, integration was achieved.

When more than 90 percent of a corporation's share value was attributable to tangible assets, accounting systems were critical management tools. Today, when intangible assets contribute more than 80 percent of the shareholder worth in technology-driven companies, it only makes sense to manage those intangible assets with the same vigor.

If you witnessed the evolution of integrated accounting solutions, think déjà vu. If you're one of the newer generation IT managers, you're about to have a history lesson—one that will help shape the future of IPAMs.

Following is an overview of the acronyms that you are likely to encounter.

IPAM: Intellectual Property and Asset Management System. Recently, we've found IPAM becoming more like the kitchen drawer—everything having to do with software related to patents, trademarks, or intellectual property in general was being labeled an "IPAM."

What it means: The word *management,* when used in relation to intellectual property, usually means *money.* It makes sense that such a management solution keeps track of maintenance fees and licensing payments (expense), royalty payments (income), or valuation (tax reporting). Many of these management tasks have historically been out-sourced to intellectual property management companies, which, for a hefty commission or activity-based fee, would make the necessary payments on your behalf and track and report the financial activity related to your intellectual property.

One critical value component to managing intellectual property, your patents and trademarks, is the timely payment of periodic maintenance fees to keep each patent or trademark in force. In the United States, a patent maintenance fee on each patent must be paid at 3.5, 7.5, and 11.5 years after the patent issues. Multiply this by 100 or 1,000 patents issued to some companies every year, add to that another 50 percent for foreign-filed patents (with different maintenance fee rules for each country), and you have the kind of data that serious solutions are meant for—and the liability if your installed solution results in lost intellectual property.

An IPAM may also allow patent or trademark database searching, "temp file directories" for transaction histories or downloaded digital copies of issued patents (and track the per-copy payment), or any number of other function-specific add-on or plug-in modules.

So, while full integration within an IPAM solution is not quite here, certain functional modules developed and supported by emerging publishers can certainly be integrated to help companies reduce the management fees currently being paid to outside firms and realize some level of increased efficiency within the organization.

IP-IDAMS: Intellectual Property Integrated Data Analysis and Management System. For every problem, there is a solution. For years, the solution for managers or patent counsel wanting patent-related analysis was to contract out to a specialty intellectual property or consulting firm.

In the late 1990s, a few software companies introduced their offerings in style and a little before their time. Their patent analysis solutions commanded upward of $100,000 (plus various user fees), but to their credit, these pioneers did provide an introduction to patent data visualization that started the rush. Data analysis was coined *patent mapping* or *patent topography* because the patent data distribution was displayed to look like a topographic map.

Put to use in various configurations, the IP-IDAMS can be strategically used by department managers (1) to find new business opportunities through licensing your existing patents, (2) to discover gaps in a competitor's patent strategy that could be exploited, or (3) to plan the deployment of a patent picket fence to close in a competitor's most important patents.

Data mining and analysis of course requires data. A unique attribute of intellectual property data is that it's never all there. About 200 of the world's countries have some sort of intellectual property issuing authority—for trademarks, patents, industrial designs, and so forth. It's unlikely that all of this data will be available in one spot in the foreseeable future, so it is important to understand the various departments' requirements for quantity, data source (country), or quality of the data that may be available for data mining while assessing IP-IDAMS. At the forefront of combining searchable global patent data and IPAM software is the ERP solution from PatentCafe *(http://ERP.patentcafe.com)*.

As the various department managers begin to understand and apply the data mining power and functionality of IP-IDAMS, and bring their application needs to the PQM Team, the IT manager will help sort out the best corporatewide solution.

Who Owns the IPAM?

IT managers and CFOs wrestled with this question regarding integrated accounting systems. IT managers and engineering VPs wrestled over the question of who owns the CAD system. Now, here comes the patent/trademark/legal/intangible asset management system, with the engineering, marketing, legal, and accounting managers following down the hall behind it.

Common sense tells us that there will be excellent single-function tools that each of these departments would like, yet a one-size-fits-all solution is sure to leave some groups wanting more. It is up to the CEO to appoint the purchasing authority for the company's IPAM solution, to the CFO to perform the cost/benefit analysis of the investment, and to the IT manager to determine system qualification, vendor qualification, maintenance, user access, and system integrity.

It appears there's no single owner, which highlights the importance of the entire PQM Team working together to objectively assess the needs of each of the department managers, assess the software budget (which includes the cost of licenses, training, hardware, support personnel, and so forth), and ensure that the decisions reflect a sensitivity to the overall intangible asset management goals: increase shareholder value.

System Selection and Functional Qualification

Once each department manager weighs in with functional wish lists, it will be up to the IT manager to perform the first level of solution/vendor qualification. This may be new territory in some aspects, but the same general rules that apply to solution assessment apply to IPAMs: ability to meet functional requirements, hardware/software requirements, user training requirements, license fees, upgrades, tech/user support and costs.

Here are some of the more focused questions to ask an IPAM vendor:

- Does the IPAM solution provide patent or trademark data searching or data mining capabilities? If so, how many patents/trademarks are available from which issuing authorities (countries)? As a general metric, there are about 40 million searchable patent records from about 80 countries and about 20 million trademark records available for online search.

- What types of data and metadata are available through the system?

- How are security and firewall penetrations handled when users need to access an outside database for patent or trademark searching or data mining?

- Does the system have patent analytics capabilities? If so, do they reside on the vendor's application server, or installed on your server, behind the firewall?

- What functional modules are available now, and what modules will be available in the near/distant future? (i.e., Is there a trademark analysis module for marketing managers to conduct analysis on competitors' brand management strategies, or an integrated docketing system that will allow your corporate counsel to communicate directly with outside counsel?)

- How easy is the system to learn? Will you be required to conduct user training for all employees who need to access the IPAM system? (Hint: Forget the canned demo and ask for a demo account. Then let the various users/managers simply sit and work the system without training. Intuitive, practical systems will rise to the top of the short list.)

- How is the system paid for (what is the pricing model)? Nearly every system will have some monthly or per-seat license component, as well as a pay-per-use component for special features, analytical models, patent downloads, and other optional features.

- What system management/system administration capabilities does the system have (remember, you may be administering this system)?

Develop a feature list, provide it to your vendors, and ask them to indicate how their solution compares against this list. Distribute the vendor information that you gather to other department managers during your PQM meetings, and as a team, decide which IPAM will likely deliver the necessary functionality within the available budget. Then carry this system forward for your organization.

System Modules

Although it is impossible to predict what future functionality will find its way into an IPAM system, we can at least give a quick listing of the functionality currently available, either as a standalone product or as part of an integrated IPAM solution. This list may provide a starting point to begin your assessment:

- Patent search engine
- Trademark search engine
- Patent analytics/patent mapping and visualization tools
- Trademark mapping or analysis tools
- Licensing royalty/annuity tracking systems
- Intellectual property maintenance fees payment scheduling
- Legal docketing system
- Electronic patent or trademark filing system
- Portal services (i.e., streaming (into your intranet), articles, resources, third-party services or products such as intellectual property insurance, loans, document retrieval services, and so forth)
- Web-distributed application: patent work flow
- Knowledge management/IA: user knowledge base/transaction recording
- Patent, trademark, or intangible asset valuation analysis
- Web-distributed application: patent drawing system
- Technical journal/nonpatent database search or meta search modules
- Patent/technology licensing module (for promotion of technology available for license)
- Applications that may use a client/server configuration

Information Access and Liability

Managing access to patent-related data is set by your company's policy as determined by the PQM Team. This policy may be based on several factors, including your company's legal philosophy regarding patents and patent searching, your company's product and software development methodologies (resulting in patents), and even the company's budget.

Internal Access Privileges/Security Levels

IT managers are already aware of the measures in place to limit or monitor employee access to sensitive data, so we're not going to start from square one; however, compared to the system you have in place now, you should be aware of some new access levels, the different types of people who will be accessing your IPAM, and the need to develop internal systems that will allow you to monitor security throughout the new IPAM system.

Because an integrated intellectual property (IP) solution consists of modules specific to certain departments, managers, or employees, the modules should be available only on a basis of need. For instance, marketing managers may need access to the patent analysis tools that will allow them to create competitive analysis reports, but they do not need access to the legal docketing system.

In addition to the obvious security access levels that must be set up internally, IPAM systems can tie users in your organization with nodes on an extranet, such as your outside corporate or patent attorneys or outside vendors. It is critical that diligent monitoring of authorized access is in place. Although it is somewhat easier for HR to notify the IT manager when an employee leaves (notice to disable access), it is almost impossible to monitor the employee attrition of outside users who have password access.

We're not going to suggest methods to address every conceivable security access scenario, but we do hope that this notice will alert you to issues that may differ from your current security measures.

Many of the features available through an IPAM have direct legal implications, and it is important to be aware of these before your organ-

ization experiences a loss of intellectual property. It is important for corporate counsel to advise all managers on the legal implications associated with the implementation of an IPAM, the security policy with
respect to labor laws, or any other applicable laws of your jurisdiction.

Intellectual Property Liability Exposure

You're not a lawyer, you don't need to be. You do, however, need to be
made aware of how IT plays an increasingly important role in reducing
the possibility of the company's exposure to what would ultimately be
quantified as a financial loss. To craft a department policy that will help
the entire IT department reduce the company's potential loss of intellectual property, the IT manager will need to sit down with corporate
counsel and discuss all of the points of exposure to the possible loss of IP.
Before you ask your attorneys for advice, however, you may want to have
a broad understanding of how IT-related activities can increase or
decrease the exposure to loss. It is up to the IT manager to educate corporate counsel as to possible exposure points; they will take it from there.

Here are a few areas where poor or nonexistent intellectual property management policies may result in loss (and corporate counsel may
identify many more):

- *IPAM systems that contain engineering drawings, new technology
  sketches, or other information about the company's future technology
  direction.* Patent work flow systems, Web-distributed drafting
  programs, or electronic patent filing systems fall into this category. **Exposure:** employee theft, hackers

- *Patent licensing/royalty annuity tracking systems that maintain an
  accounting of royalties paid (or are payable) under a license agreement.*
  Exposure: loss of audit trail, possible loss of royalty revenue if
  the system loses a licensee

- *Patent and trademark maintenance fee payment scheduling system (or
  docketing system).* These systems are, in essence, legal calendars

on which the timely management, next activities, or next government fee payments are scheduled. **Exposure:** bugs, installation problems, crashes or loss of data in calendars can result in missed payment or response schedules, and total invalidation and loss of patent or trademark rights

- *Patent infringement.* Although this topic is covered in more depth later in this chapter, it's important to understand that with the incredible number of patents being issued on software, the probability that even the IT department may find itself on the defensive end of a patent infringement suit is growing. Seemingly innocent programming by members of the IT department is not a defense for infringement. There exists an increasing possibility that code written internally for critical factory processes such as semiconductor wafer quality analysis or process sequences for robotic assembly of products your company manufactures may infringe issued software patents. **Exposure:** patent infringement claims with a possible injunction that could shut down your company's production line or internal processes, software product recalls, financial damages awards

To properly address liability issues related to software and potential loss of intellectual property, it's advisable to include HR, engineering, programmers and system administrators, and most important, your corporate attorney in all discussions. Without the team approach to intellectual property security, it's likely that significant holes in a policy will remain, and with it, the exposure to actions that may be brought on by the shareholders for any loss in stock value associated with loss of intellectual property value that they might suffer.

Software Patents

Software patents are usually thought of as those applications developed by computer and dot-com Internet companies and used as the foundation of their business, but the breadth and influence of software patents in other environments is becoming increasingly evident. Today, they can pervade and influence every department within the organization, including manufacturing, marketing, finance, IT, and even shipping, receiving, and warehousing.

Patents Changing the IT Landscape

Software patents may be a curious novelty to many in the IT sector, even though every IT manager worth his or her salt has heard about the Amazon one-click method and the Priceline.com name-your-own-price patents. It is vitally important that IT managers get patent proficient—and quickly. Patents may be a foreign concept to many IT managers in non-technical businesses such as multilevel marketing and commodity manufacturers (such as woolen socks or ice cream), but they loom large as a business tool that could lead to a changing landscape regardless of the industry sector or business type.

We have included a few patent claims from recently issued software patents in the In the Real World section to illustrate the breadth of ownership of software functionality a patent holder may wind up with. Familiarize yourself with what's happening in the software patent arena by simply studying issued patents on processes, methods, and algorithms.

Thousands of pages have been written on software patent subject matter, so we're not going to drill into the technical, legal, or social issues associated with software patents in a single chapter. Those interested in learning more about software patents can find plenty of material. It is important, however, for every IT manager to walk away from this chapter with an understanding of how software patents, or the lack of them, could significantly affect overall company operations and shareholder value. Once IT managers grasp how software patents fit into their organization, they should schedule a meeting with corporate counsel or senior staff to discuss the potential vulnerabilities or opportunities associated with software patents in the organization.

Together with proper legal and business counsel, the IT manager can begin crafting a patent software policy.

Offense/Defense

Corporate counsel can advise IT managers of the legal nuances of software patents. For now, however, we're simply going to address software patents from a business perspective—those that help a company establish either a defensive or offensive patent posture.

A *defensive posture* is one in which the IT manager takes care to search, then has the corporate patent counsel search, for issued patents related to the software programs that the IT manager is planning on developing. This defensive posture may include searching patents related to Website features, if the IT manager is attempting to develop a unique way customers can conduct e-commerce transactions. It may include an analysis of patents issued for assembly line controllers for the factory, so that the program that the IT department comes up with will not result in infringement of another company's patent.

Making the entire programming department more aware of software patents will not only help a company avoid possible patent infringement issues, but software patents that teach various solutions can often spur on the development of the next evolution of software functionality.

An *offensive posture* is one in which the IT manager determines that a new program may indeed be novel, functional, and not obvious, and therefore elects to obtain a patent on it. When the IT manager believes that a certain program could be awarded a patent, the PQM Team must convene and determine the potential benefit the program could bring to the company (i.e., a process that speeds up the production line, a unique method of e-commerce customer interface, or other program that could result in any kind of competitive advantage). If the advantages are clear and can justify the budget to prepare and file the patent (business justified), then the company's patent attorney will address the invention documentation process, and will begin preparing the patent application.

IT managers should keep in mind not only that company processes or software products may qualify for patent protection, but also that even inventive processes arbitrarily developed (such as the use of advertising logos and a screen saver) may become important and valuable additions to the company's intellectual property portfolio.

A final consideration is the added value that a patent may have as a defensive tool. Quite often, one company will file an infringement suit against another company for patent infringement; however, after the arduous legal maneuvering is finished, both companies may settle by cross-licensing their patents. In other words, if your company has a valuable software patent, in the event that a company claims infringement on its patent, you have created a bargaining chip for licensing negotiations, in addition to the other obvious patent ownership benefits we've already discussed.

Corporate Technology Exchange
Internet Access to Corporate Licensable Technology

If a picture is worth a thousand words, then a quick look at the General Electric Company's patent licensing Website at *www.GEpatents.com* shows you that it would fill a book. This is the embodiment of how a company can exploit the Internet to promote licensing of its patent portfolio.

Because Website development often falls under the purview of the IT department, it may be the IT department that drives the initiative.

Patenting a Web Site

In July 1998, when the U.S. Court of Appeals for the Federal Circuit ruled on *State Street Bank & Trust* v. *Signature Financial Group, Inc.*, it held that a computer program for a "Hub and Spoke Financial Services Configuration" is patentable subject matter. The invention in the State Street Bank case blew the doors to software patents wide open. Reading more software patents will help the IT manager develop patent consciousness. Here is claim number one of the Amazon.com one-click patent:

US Patent Number: 5,960,411

We claim:

1. A method of placing an order for an item comprising:

under control of a client system,

displaying information identifying the item; and

in response to only a single action being performed, sending a request to order the item along with an identifier of a purchaser of the item to a server system;

under control of a single-action ordering component of the server system,

receiving the request;

retrieving additional information previously stored for the purchaser identified by the identifier in the received request; and

generating an order to purchase the requested item for the purchaser identified by the identifier in the received request using the retrieved additional information; and fulfilling the generated order to complete purchase of the item whereby the item is ordered without using a shopping cart ordering model.

Amazon is not alone in patenting Internet-based software. Stop by the flight schedule screen at the Southwest Airlines Website at *www.southwest.com* and see if you can locate the patent-pending notice at the bottom. Are you planning on programming an online order form anytime soon? Clearly, software patents apply to *every* business.

Although someone other than the IT manager will make the determination to promote licensable technology via the Web, there are a few things the IT manager can bring to the discussion:

- *Marketing and promotion.* It is true that the Internet can be an incredibly cost-effective marketing channel through which to promote licensable technology, but the fact remains that unless that Website is properly promoted, listed, and placed well in the major search engines, it will do little good in getting the technology in front of interested licensees. If your organization isn't fortunate enough to have a Website like IBM, HP, GE, or another large company that generates a high visitor traffic count, you may recommend to the staff that they look at some of these Internet marketing alternatives:

    - Listing the technology on Websites that are already getting very high traffic—Websites designed specifically to promote licensing intellectual property. Here is a list of many of the popular technology transfer Websites operating at the time of this writing: *www.2XFR.com, www.uventures.com, www.pl-x.com, www.yet2.com, www.patex.com, www.ipex.com, www.techex.com*

- Listing on commercial tech transfer Web sites can be advantageous, but it sometimes involves a contract that provides the Web site owner with a commission or transaction fee of up to $50,000 if a patent is licensed through that brokerage, so review the fine print.

- Obtaining a branded front end to a technology transfer Web site that is seeing high traffic numbers. This option has the benefit of (1) keeping your technologies and your brand in front of the visitor once they find your Web site, and (2) gives your technology higher exposure since the licensable patents are searchable in the host technology transfer Web site as well.

- *Make versus Buy.* Given the pros and cons of building a corporate patent licensing Web site versus having a tech transfer host build a branded version of an existing technology exchange, the IT manager should be prepared to explore and assess alternatives, along with price, technical, and development schedule considerations. Two companies offering this higher branded visibility for companies that also want the high visitor traffic are PatentCafé, with its patent licensing marketplace at *www.2XFR.com/branded.asp,* and PLX Systems, Inc. at *www.pl-x.com.*

  Another benefit to integrating your technology into a branded version of an existing commercial technology transfer Web site is that you dovetail onto a robust, tested design that may include database, industry standard search taxonomy, intuitive user interface, and other proven design and administration features for the patent owner.

  If the IT manager is responsible for the Internet-based promotion of a company's technology and opts for a branded front end to an existing technology transfer database, they should expect more than a simple color change and a "look-and feel-alike" page. The IT manager should provide to the database host a template page from the company's Website that incorporates all of the desired navigation buttons to ensure a seamless transition from the technology transfer pages to other pages in the corporate Website.

At this point, you are armed with a working knowledge of the patent system relative to the IT department and can address IPAM systems, patent security issues related to a digital communications platform, software patents, liability and risk reduction, and now, patent licensing exchanges. You are ready to become an invaluable member of the PQM Team.

CHAPTER 11

Patent Management and the Corporate/ IP Counsel

After reading this chapter you will be able to

- Understand the important role of the corporate patent attorney in today's business environment
- Learn how the patent attorney can enhance the company's PQM intranet
- Understand the attorney's role in supporting department needs

This chapter speaks to the corporate intellectual property counsel and addresses the increasingly important role of the corporate patent attorney in today's business environment. Not only do IP counselors handle patent filing and prosecution as they have for decades, they are now required to assist with the growing responsibilities of managing intangible assets, which, for many high-technology companies, account for more than 85 percent of the market value.

If you are not already doing so, you should begin to fit the *new* role and address the issues that you should consider while securing the value (for shareholders) of corporate information and knowledge through legal means, and in particular the corporate patent portfolio.

The responsibility to manage corporate patent assets starts at the top with the CEO by adopting a PQM strategy and initiating PQM teams. It begins there as a business-wise decision, but corporate counsel and patent counsel provide critical input into these activities because they will play an important part from the legal side.

Legal Tender

Intellectual property is increasingly becoming legal tender, the new monetary unit for technology-driven companies. So too is corporate/patent counsel becoming increasingly responsible as the legal tender (i.e., tending to the corporation's intellectual property/patent portfolio and intangible assets and the impact on shareholder value).

Increased Standard of Practice

In the wake of the Enron collapse, SEC scrutiny of accounting standards and the advent of FAS-142 financial reporting of the value of intangible assets, as well as the strategic and tactical use of litigation, interference, reissues, licensing, and so forth, what new standards of practice must the corporate IP counsel rise to in order to maintain a strong corporate posture and to preserve shareholder value?

Although new *legal* standards of practice may evolve (ongoing proposed legislation regarding disclosure and reporting requirements as proposed by various federal agencies), in a more practical sense, corporate IP attorneys today are facing a higher level of performance expectation by the shareholders. Here are some of the duties that will require corporate counsel's contribution, assuming that companies adopt a corporatewide PQM program:

- Patent work flow: Managing the invention process
- Leverage IP for corporate gain, competitive advantage, and shareholder value
- Strategy
- Competitive intelligence, focused innovation
- M&A, due diligence
- Promote corporate innovation development

Patent Work Flow: Managing the Invention Process

The examples used in this chapter will focus on the use of patents as the mode of protecting intangible property; however, the concepts are applicable or analogous to the other means of protection such as trade secrets, trademarks, copyrights, and proprietary information. Although the word *corporate* typically refers to a for-profit enterprise, much of the discussion in this chapter applies to many nonprofit entities such as universities.

A responsibility exists to educate, promote, and monitor the process from concept to patent application and beyond. Patent corporate counsel's role is to capture and quantify intellectual capital that can be converted into the most valuable patents.

Today, CEOs, Wall Street analysts, shareholders, and certainly all who are involved in technology are aware of the importance and value of patents and of protecting corporate information and knowledge. IP counsel bears a large part of the responsibility to ensure that the corporation protects its assets with quality patents and, at times, discouraging the pursuit of frivolous patents, which can become a costly exercise in futility.

Most often, but not uniformly, the team that is tasked to develop and manage the patent portfolio is within a legal department, the group that will be called on to manage and execute disputes related to patents and other IP, and more specifically the IP counsel. The IP counsel is almost always a patent attorney, although the level of corporate skills demanded has increased dramatically over the past seven to ten years. The increased ability and need for a commercial enterprise to use intellectual properties, such as patents, as exploitable business assets has required this expanded umbrella of responsibilities of the IP counsel.

Exhibit 11.1 maps a typical invention disclosure process that captures the inventor's innovation in a form that can then be reviewed and processed by the PQM Team.

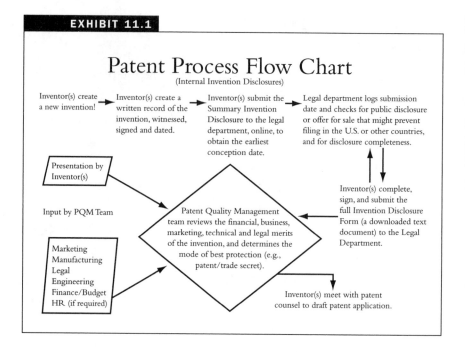

Patent Process Flow Chart
(Internal Invention Disclosures)

Inventor(s) create a new invention! → Inventor(s) create a written record of the invention, witnessed, signed and dated. → Inventor(s) submit the Summary Invention Disclosure to the legal department, online, to obtain the earliest conception date. → Legal department logs submission date and checks for public disclosure or offer for sale that might prevent filing in the U.S. or other countries, and for disclosure completeness.

Presentation by Inventor(s)

Input by PQM Team

Marketing
Manufacturing
Legal
Engineering
Finance/Budget
HR (if required)

Patent Quality Management team reviews the financial, business, marketing, technical and legal merits of the invention, and determines the mode of best protection (e.g., patent/trade secret).

Inventor(s) complete, sign, and submit the full Invention Disclosure Form (a downloaded text document) to the Legal Department.

Inventor(s) meet with patent counsel to draft patent application.

Leverage IP for Corporate Gain, Competitive Advantage, and Shareholder Value

Stated broadly, the mission of the corporate IP counsel and his or her immediate team is to strategically promote, capture, manage, and protect (offensively and defensively) corporate innovations for a competitive advantage:

- *Promote.* The corporation's counsel plays the role of supporting the patent promotion in such cases as licensing in, licensing out, and cross-licensing. Thus corporate counsel's responsibility to ensure adequate breadth and scope of quality patents is paramount.

- *Capture.* During the term of employment, an employee will receive compensation in return for his or her contributions and work, often exemplified as intellectual property or intellectual capital. Patent counsel, in working with HR, must ensure that the company captures the intellectual capital produced by the employees and that this knowledge contribution remains with the company after the employee leaves.

- *Manage.* Patents must be filed in a timely manner. Strategy and tactics must be used that are consistent with corporate PQM objectives. Patent applications must be prosecuted, PCTs filed, CIPs filed, and appeals pursued as required. If maintenance fees are paid by legal counsel, then these too must be monitored. All these elements fall under legal time restraints that must be honored, or else patent rights may be lost forever.

- *Protect.* Corporate counsel is expected to seek out and litigate against infringers, as well as protect the company from claims of infringement. This requires an objective approach to infringement and litigation alternatives, because occasionally the litigation costs can exceed the value of the IP being litigated.

Strategy

A determining factor of the success of any organization is the degree to which the goals of that organization are integrated within all of its activities. For corporate IP counsel, the strategies and operational tactics of the IP function must be closely aligned with, contribute to, and inform the business goals of the corporate enterprise as a whole. This goal necessitates positive and frequent communication with many often nonintegrated corporate and operational business functions.

IP counsel may well find her or himself in the only position of knowledge transfer between certain groups; an IP counsel with vision and a good understanding of the corporate goals can play a critical role in achieving those goals in more efficient and creative ways. As discussed in great depth in Chapter 3, the strategy your corporation has developed should be reflected in your corporate counsel's decisions and actions.

Competitive Intelligence and Focused Innovation

As IP counsel, you should have the expertise needed to discover and, more important, analyze the inventions of current and potential competitors. Much information is publicly available to bring competitive and precompetitive knowledge to your attention, including patent search and IPAM software and analytics. When a competing technology is discovered, you must determine the qualification of the breadth of the patents. In order to make decisions consistent with your PQM strategy and to the benefit of your company's shareholders, your IP counsel will be the qualifier. You may also become aware of certain competitive technologies available to license in, based in part on a licensing agency such as LES or simply by being active in your field.

Promote Corporate Innovation Development

Just as the IP functions must be aligned with the business goals of the corporation, to be most successful the organization must develop and maintain a culture wherein innovation is fostered and those who invent for the benefit of the corporation are honored, respected, and rewarded. It falls to the IP counsel to champion this cause and to enlist and educate as co-champions both senior executives and product-level managers. Management buy-in has been a significant hurdle to many an IP counsel. Because innovation has a long time horizon, it is often well below the radar and often considered an important but not urgent matter within those corporations that focus on quarterly earnings as an indicator of success. Will the new FASB rules, SEC reporting requirements, and loudly voiced shareholder expectations come together as the catalyst that finally grabs the attention of the CEO and causes the top-down implementation of a PQM program?

Shareholders and Corporations Win

IP counsel should be able to provide and explain the business justifications not just for protecting intellectual property, but also for developing a strategy and process for managing a patent portfolio; education and awareness training should be provided to executives, managers, and all potential

IN THE REAL WORLD

The PQM Plan

Theory is fine until the CEO wants you to provide a comprehensive report that can be included in the shareholder report. That's where the rubber meets the road. To kick start your IP program structure, we've compiled a short list of items and issues that you should be addressing at some level. Take the test, and see if you:

____ Periodically take inventory of the corporate IP portfolio (IP audit)

____ Assess and rank by market valuation

____ Fill out web-based invention disclosure forms

____ Use decision-making metrics for invention disclosures

____ Employ embedded stage-gate processes to capture innovation where it occurs

____ Focus innovation and development to increase yield of valuable IP

____ Determine technology weaknesses within corporate and competitors

____ Provide incentives for inventions related to corporate business

____ Minimize loss of proprietary and confidential information (information protection)

____ Reduce maintenance fee costs by abandoning noncore IP

____ Derive revenue by bundling and selling or licensing noncore IP and by licensing IP for applications outside core

____ Minimize patent and trademark prosecution expenses by bringing work in-house

____ Supply competitive intelligence on industry innovation to R&D

____ Work with R&D to design around competitor's patents

____ Use patent analysis tools to anticipate competitor technology development trends

____ Raise awareness of IP infringement within marketing and sales groups

____ Establish best defensive posture against claims of infringement and misappropriation of third-party IP

inventors. The advantages to the corporation should be made clear. Following are several of these advantages and opportunities, each of which calls for tactical implementation tailored to the particular organization:

- Protect and prolong a competitive advantage by filing a patent application on the inventions behind or embodied in that advantage.

- Encapsulate and more easily protect investments made in R&D by turning the knowledge created into a proprietary business asset.

- Minimize wasted R&D efforts that may result in a claim of patent infringement by a third-party patent holder by looking at the publications (patents and literature) of established and emerging companies working on similar problems. With this knowledge early in the process, R&D can be redirected or a workaround can be designed. The intelligence information gathered could suggest obtaining a license under the third-party patent, obtaining a noninfringement or invalidity opinion of counsel, or even identifying a potential acquisition target.

- Ensure freedom of design and development by publishing internal innovations and inventions in trade journals or at conferences.

By adding to the public domain, the right of maintaining the invention exclusively to the corporation is lost, but the hopes of others to secure a similar proprietary position are often spoiled.

- Provide opportunities for cross-licensing of technologies. In many technology-based industries, a patent portfolio is used as a means of détente, with broad threats of patent infringement claims resulting most often in bringing the parties to a settlement whereby each grants to the other a license under some portion of their patent portfolio. A company that has a thin portfolio may not be able to ante up to that challenge and will suffer the choice between paying royalty fees or litigating a patent infringement suit.

- Enhance the company's reputation for innovation. One measure of the innovativeness of a company is the number of patents awarded in its name each year. This number is reported

---

IN THE REAL WORLD

Top 10 Organizations Receiving Most Patents in 2001

Rank	# Patents	Company
1	3,411	International Business Machines (IBM)
2	1,953	NEC Corporation
3	1,877	Canon Kabushiki Kaisha
4	1,643	Micron Technology, Inc.
5	1,450	Samsung Electronics Co. Ltd.
6	1,440	Matsushita Electrical Industrial Co. Ltd.
7	1,363	Sony Corporation
8	1,271	Hitachi, Ltd.
9	1,184	Mitsubishi Denki Kabushiki Kaisha
10	1,166	Fujitsu Limited

Source: U.S. Patent & Trademark Office

annually by the U.S. Patent and Trademark Office. The companies at the top of that list gain goodwill and an enhanced reputation in the eyes of its customers as well as its corporate peers. This recognition by an unbiased third party is an added tool for the marketing and sales functions.

- Earn royalty income. The ability to exclude another company from exploiting a product (device), process, or method that is considered to be enabling or optimal to success in that industry gives the patent holder the option to exclude the competitor completely or to charge a royalty for practicing the invention as claimed in the patent. Essentially, the patent holder or corporation is now able to participate in the market not only through the successes of its own sales efforts, but to some extent also through the successes of others. Thus, in the instance of a patent on broad enabling technology where the patent holder cannot service the entire market for the invention, it may well make more financial sense to license widely under the patent to maximize the number of royalty-paying entities rather than using the patent to exclude all others. Chapters 3 and 7 discuss in depth the PQM strategy that makes your product the industry standard. There is no better or more profitable way to do this than through licensing out your patented technology.

- Realize untapped savings and income. One important role of managing a patent portfolio that began receiving popular attention in the mid-1990s is known as mining the patent portfolio. The premise behind this is twofold: (1) corporations often lose track of the relevance of individual patents in their portfolio, and (2) some of those individual patents no longer have relevance to the current business goals. The entire patent portfolio would be reviewed for a reality check, and those patents determined to be no longer relevant would be licensed, assigned, or donated to others. At a minimum, the patent would be abandoned country by country at its next scheduled maintenance fee payment to avoid what would have been a wasted expense. Auditing a company's licensees under its patent portfolio became in vogue around the same time. The purpose of this audit is to ensure that any royalties due to a corporation by its licensees are in fact being paid by those licensees. These royalties are essentially found money going straight to the bottom line.

Promotion: Incentives

Many successful intellectual property management programs foster and exist in an environment where there is an expectation that inventions are a natural result of expenses directed to R&D efforts, and in fact, the whole commercialization process from concept through final commer-

 TIPS & TECHNIQUES

Did you know that there is a new generation of intellectual property management software tools to help you better control and manage your intellectual property? From robust international patent searching to patent analysis and mapping, competitive analysis trending, patent work flow management, docketing, and patent application preparation software, just about any efficiency tool that you need is becoming available. For a sampling, see the following Websites:

www.firsttofile.com, digital patent work flow

www.foundationIP.com, digital patent work flow

www.IPSearchEngine.com, global patent search and analytics, valuation

www.IPDox.com, Web-based docketing program

www.pl-x.com, IP management, valuation, and asset mining

www.2XFR.com, corporate branded patent licensing exchange

cialization. It is a natural assumption that unless this expectation is communicated throughout the organization, there simply will not be a continual stream of innovation and patents to feed into an increasingly valuable portfolio. In contrast, many other companies have a well or poorly understood standardized approach to product development from concept to commercialization—with varying outcomes.

Whatever the present corporate approach may be to innovation, a thorough PQM approach will be more effective and have specific outcomes. With a qualified PQM strategy, the IP counsel plays an important part of that work flow at several potential points of invention. For instance, a question to be answered by a project manager at a given stage of development may be as simple as: "What competitive advantage has been added during this stage, and what makes it advantageous?" The answer to this question should be discussed in actual dialogue between the project manager and IP counsel.

The IP counsel should ensure that the corporation provides meaningful incentives to those who invent and to the managers of those inventors. The invention disclosure is not the end, but rather the beginning of a process that requires some valuable time from the inventor. Employees rightfully prioritize according to the priorities of the organization, and those priorities are most tangibly communicated in the form of bonuses, management objectives, and promotions. If inventing is to feel like a useful activity and if department managers are to give their PQM teams the space to innovate, the IP counsel must be these managers' advocates in developing and championing these processes.

The inventor should not be put in the position of choosing whether to work with patent counsel to speed the patent process and get an earlier filing and perhaps issue date; this cooperation should be expected as a policy of PQM. Most corporate patent incentive or award policies provide a bonus to the inventor at certain milestones; for instance, submission of an invention disclosure that results in a patent or trade secret, upon filing a patent application (after helping patent counsel draft the application), and upon issuance of the subsequent patent to issue from application.

Chapter 9 (Human Resources) covers establishing, communicating, conducting, and maintaining inventor awards and incentives programs.

Innovation Web Site: Your PQM Intranet

Enterprise level companies were quick to learn the advantages of building and maintaining a corporate Intranet—an "Internet" network intended for use by company employees, usually inside corporate facilities. The list of benefits continue to grow with each new application, but Intranets have been responsible for instant communication to employees by HR regarding changes in 401 programs, health and dental programs, telecommuting, and updates to tax withholding forms.

Intranets also serve as a knowledge base wherein companies can offer a repository of white papers, technical publications, journals, internal research notes, and more.

As intellectual property management continues to grow in importance to corporations, so does the necessity of building and maintaining an innovation Web site—a portal of information specifically selected and packaged to support the development, capture, protection, and exploitation of intellectual capital and invention.

An innovation Web site should include, among other information, expert articles on patents and licensing, the latest intellectual property books and journals, online forms (non-disclosure agreements, employee confidential disclosures, patent forms, and so forth), as well as access to IPAM software, gateway through the firewall to searchable patent databases.

In a PQM environment, the innovation Web site becomes more of an important educational and training tool. Marketing, manufacturing, sales, engineering, legal, and finance departments all have an ongoing need for support and encouragement to maintain the momentum of the PQM system. They should also come to rely on the innovation Web site as the knowledge hub for their PQM activities.

Training and Education

Contrary to an attorney's first rule of practice, education and training of employees *does* require counsel to commit its advice and direction to writing. One of the best ways to manage written material is to put it in one place where it can be managed and changed instantly: the company's innovation Web site. As IP counsel, you can play a huge role in a new PQM system by contributing to the innovation Web site.

What does the marketing manager do if an inventor contacts him or her with a proposal to submit an invention for company consideration? How do you provide your engineering group with a steady stream of information about reading patents to identify licensable technology, without having them get into the legal aspects of a patent document? How should the marketing group incorporate patent, copyright, and trademark notices on marketing and sales materials?

Today, in most instances, employees who encounter these issues will wing it—a dangerous practice because one slip can expose the company to a lawsuit that will negatively impact shareholder value.

Educating marketing and engineering personnel on what constitutes infringement, how to safeguard confidential information, and how to leverage intellectual property knowledge for competitive advantage is an ongoing task, not a single event. It is an inherent outcome of the establishment and launching of your company's PQM system. Incorporating downloadable master forms such as invention disclosures, submission and nonconfidential letters, employee forms (for the HR department), patent database access for research, intellectual property–related news and events, and listings of intellectual property for license are all examples of content that should be provided throughout the organization.

Clearly, the time has come for the corporate IP Web site. While PQM team members from marketing, engineering, HR, operations, and finance will all have their hand in structuring the content on the IP Web site, corporate counsel finalizes and approves the legal content and its subsequent changes.

Capturing Innovation

All of this promotion and awareness training can be rendered inconsequential if there is no clear and simple process for capturing and transferring the invention from the mind of the inventor into a decision process whereby inventions are considered worthy of protection, whether that be as a patent, trade secret, or defensive publication. Hence, a company's HR department must have the appropriate legal forms ready for execution by new and existing employees, forms that have been reviewed or provided by corporate counsel.

Analytic Decision Process

Deciding what inventions should be pursued aggressively and which ones should probably be abandoned (or publicly disclosed to prevent patenting by a competitor) is not an arbitrary task. Without an objective process, the PQM team and corporate counsel will be unable to apply evaluation consistency to every invention. The decisions about what inventions to protect, and which ones not to, can be influenced by end-of-quarter profits, corporate downsizing, acquisition of another company (and its portfolio), or a host of other factors that have little to do with the independent charter of the PQM Team. Exhibit 11.2 provides a view of one decision process that can be applied to almost every corporate environment. The upper right box indicates the most urgent intellectual property activity (file a patent), while the left column and lower row present the more casual action items.

Supporting Department Needs: Forms, Policies, and Systems

As corporate patent counsel, it is your job to support other cross-functional department needs with regard to patent and intellectual property

EXHIBIT 11.2

Invention Protection/Filing Decision Chart

Ability to Exclude Competitors

			High	Medium	Low
HIGH Applicability to competitors: Significant Scope of claims: Broad (difficult to invent around) Enforceable/willing to enforce: Yes Infringement detection: Easy Alternative approaches: Few known			Offensive Filing to Control Competitor Activity Consider Licensing Broadly Filing Priority 1	Offensive Filing to Control Competitor Activity Consider Licensing Broadly Filing Priority 2	Defensive Filing (Freedom of Activity) Maintain as Trade Secret License Only Outside Fields of Use
MEDIUM Applicability to competitors: Some Scope of claims: Moderate (can invent around with some effort) Enforceable/willing to enforce: Yes Infringement detection: Probable Alternative approaches: Some known			Offensive Filing to Control Competitor Activity Consider Licensing Selectively Filing Priority 2	Offensive Filing to Control Competitor Activity Consider Licensing Selectively Filing Priority 3	Defensive Filing (Freedom of Activity) Maintain as Trade Secret License Only Outside Fields of Use
LOW Applicability to competitors: Little Scope of claims: Narrow (easy to invent around) Enforceable/willing to enforce: Uncertain Infringement detection: Difficult Alternative approaches: Many			Maintain as Trade Secret Defensive Publication Donation for Tax Deduction Know-how License	Defensive Filing (Freedom of Activity) Maintain as Trade Secret License Only Outside Fields of Use	Defensive Filing (Freedom of Activity) Maintain as Trade Secret License Only Outside Fields of Use

EXHIBIT 11.2 *(continued)*

Desire/Ability to Practice the Invention In-House

LOW	MEDIUM	HIGH
Market/volume: Small	Market/volume: Average	Market/volume: Significant
Use: Unlikely	Use: Selectively	Use: Broadly
Add-on products: Few	Add-on products: Many	Add-on products: Most
Alternate approaches: Many	Alternate approaches: Some	Alternative approaches: Few
Scope of claims: dominated by another patent	Scope of claims: optimized to related product(s)	Scope of claims: Broad, dominating
Length of use: Short	Length of use: Single product life-cycle	Length of practice: Single
		Length of use: Enduring

management. Of course, this makes sense, but many corporate patent counsel (and CEOs/ICOs) still pigeonhole patent attorneys as the patent researcher, writer, and advisor. As a PQM Team member, your role is expanding, and we have outlined a short list of how you will need to interface with other department heads:

- *Human Resources.* Provide employee invention assignment forms/employment policy language and forms related to assignment of copyrights, trade secrets, and intellectual capital.

- *Finance.* Provide support on patent valuation methods for FASB reporting, portfolio analysis, licensing calculations, and patents or IP being acquired from other companies.

- *Marketing.* Provide licensing advice, help marketing identify licensing in opportunities, review and advise on licensing agreements, new product submission agreements, and educate marketing on issues of cross-licensing and infringement avoidance.

- *CEO/ICO.* Provide litigation risk analysis, identify potential infringers, recommend litigation and licensing strategy, and establish intellectual property–related metrics that should be reported by the various department heads during weekly or monthly staff meetings.

- *Engineering.* Ensure proper document control policies, engineering notebook maintenance/indexing/archiving, training on how to read patents, and educate on the risks and value of defensive disclosures versus preservation of patent opportunity.

- *All other departments.* Conduct a department intellectual property audit to identify policies and practices that should be considered to create, capture, develop, exploit, or protect intellectual capital that may qualify for protection under a patent, trademark, copyright, or trade secret—the essence of a PQM Team:

  - Forms, policies, and systems

  - Corporate reports for executive staff and Board of Directors

  - Website (internal and external) research and educational resources

  - Policies to managing outside patent counsel

  - Continual education and training on patent quality improvement

  - Advising on compliance with ever-evolving laws as appropriate

CHAPTER 12

Patent Management Paradigm for the CEO/ICO

After reading this chapter you will be able to

- Understand the role of the CEO in terms of overall responsibility for the patent program

- Learn to create and implement a mission to meet shareholder expectations

- Learn the role of the intellectual capital officer (ICO)

- Learn how to develop, implement, and manage a Patent Quality Management (PQM) system

President Harry S. Truman set the gold standard of presidential responsibility when he coined the phrase: "The buck stops here." Now, in the shadows of Enron, Global Crossing, Worldcom, and other business catastrophes, shareholders are holding presidents and CEOs to that gold standard. You *are* where the buck stops.

If you have had reason to establish that all important top-level staff position, the intellectual capital officer (ICO), then in matters related to management of your company's patents, trademarks, and intangible assets, the ICO will stop the buck-passing.

Not long ago, corporate chiefs who led their organizations in pursuit of leading-edge technology were called visionaries. Times change. Today, only those chiefs with sharp vision will properly and profitably manage the convergence of technology, law, and business across the enterprise. This convergence defines the new value business economy; it defines intellectual asset management (IAM). We refer to this integrated management methodology as Patent Quality Management, or PQM.

So here you are, coming through one of the most tumultuous economic environments ever, and you don't have a clue how to create, develop, manage, and exploit patents as a core value component to overall business operations. Increasing shareholder value in this environment is tough for any manager; however, the smart and forward-looking CEO will manage and optimize this convergence by fostering patent development and commercialization throughout their organization.

Let's cut to the quick: You want to know the how, what, and why of launching your own patent management program. To kick-start the process, put a copy of this book in the hands of each of your top managers. Because we guide each of them to develop departmentwide patent quality management, it is relatively easy for you to delegate a management process that is introduced with consistency across the organization.

While each CEO and ICO will have his or her own ideas on what patent management program is appropriate for a particular business sector, a separate chapter has been written to speak to each and every one of your senior staff members. Each of your key managers can create, manage, or leverage patents within their respective departments—even HR, IT, and manufacturing.

We will stop short of saying that a patent-centric management core will transform your struggling company into the off-the-front contender in your industry segment, but your implementation of top-down patent management will put more distance between you and your competitors, will have a direct positive impact on revenue and profitability, and will satisfy demanding shareholders.

In 2002, the rules of business changed dramatically! It is the CEO's job (or the ICO's job, in the event the company employs an intellectual capital officer) to learn the new intellectual asset management rules and to immediately start playing the new game—to win.

Several recent books popularized the notion of extracting cash from old, forgotten patents in the company's portfolio. The reality is that more than 65 percent, and in many cases more than 90 percent, of a corporation's market value is attributable to intangible assets, and shareholders are demanding to know how corporate chiefs are managing this huge value pool. You won't be shocked to learn that most CEOs are spending significantly less than even 65 percent of their time managing the company's intangible assets, but shareholders soon will be! We suspect that most of the CEOs reading this paragraph right now fall woefully short of meeting this time management commitment.

The year 2002 was ushered in by questionable accounting practices, huge corporate failures, and a stock market that reluctantly gave up a few up-tics while overall performance pushed lower. Consumer confidence hit an all-time low, shareholder confidence in management ethics plummeted, and a new wave of criminal indictments pierced the veil of some of America's largest and most revered corporations.

Post-9/11 business was anything but business as usual, and the SEC began looking at corporate compliance with the new Financial Accounting Standards Board (FASB) Rule 142—the separate balance sheet reporting of intangible assets.

Now, shareholders are back in control, demanding performance, and this time they want quarterly improvements coupled with management practices that will withstand long-term scrutiny.

Just when we think the shifting world is becoming a little more stable, the U.S. Patent and Trademark Office launches its 21st Century Strategic Plan, which may send the cost of patents far beyond corporate planning budgets: the investment in patent applications and filing may go through the roof!

Applying patent consciousness to standard business operations as management's latest phrase of the month will do nothing to boost shareholder value, let alone instill the critical patent management knowledge needed by your senior staff members; however, by pushing PQM through the executive staff, your company will indeed develop a superior position in the knowledge economy, can boost long-term shareholder value, and will rally employees throughout the ranks to become contributing members to a new patent value-focused organization.

Meeting a Higher Standard

As the market values of many of today's leading corporations weigh in at more than 65 percent attributable to intangible assets, the old school methods of corporate and financial management simply fall short. With performance pressures mounting, shareholders, regulatory agencies, and business partners are holding CEOs to a much higher performance standard than in the recent past.

Over the past few years, more and more patent data has become available through huge databases that house global patent data. As more patent data becomes available, it is incumbent on patent researchers to dig more, qualify new technologies better, find new technologies to license in, and discover that silver bullet patent that will bring your infringement litigation to an immediate, profitable conclusion. A host of new patent analytics tools will help determine a competitor's technology investment trends, R&D focus, and intellectual property shortcomings.

CEOs wouldn't dare run a company without relying on integrated accounting software. Now that intellectual property and asset management (IPAM) system software is immediately available, CEOs must now consider implementing the best of the IPAM tools for their organization as well. Poor management practices aside, the fact is that those CEOs who embrace the enterprisewide use of the rapidly evolving software tools will overtake their competitors quickly.

Failure to meet these heightened performance standards related to intangible asset management not only jeopardizes the CEO's future with the organization, but more important, could expose the CEO to civil, possibly even criminal liability.

Patent quality management can have a direct and calculable impact on corporate competitive strength, revenue production, and long-term shareholder value-building.

A Mission that Meets Shareholder Expectations

Building shareholder value is the number-one corporate objective, so patent and intellectual property management programs must be tailored to build and support shareholder value creation.

This new economy is so important to competitive business positioning, as well as long-term shareholder value preservation and development, that the new corporate mission statement should reflect the rising importance of leveraging patents and intangible assets throughout every level of the enterprise. When was the last time you revisited your corporate mission statement?

To most people (possibly even you), patents are obtuse concepts that are difficult to really understand. We all know the words patent pending. Some of us even understand the negative impact on stock value when a patent infringement suit is launched; however, because of the elusory nature of patents, presenting a clear and concise annual report regarding patent performance is exceedingly difficult. The information must be straightforward and presented in a format that shareholders will instantly understand.

If shareholders feel that you have either failed to properly manage their patent portfolio or that your report on intangible assets was misleading, they will hold you accountable. It is time to get the tools implemented and empower your staff to leverage these tools to meet more demanding shareholder expectations.

Incorporating patents and intellectual property management into your mission statement sends a clear and resounding message through-

---

IN THE REAL WORLD

Can Aggressive IP Management Mitigate CEO's Risk?

In January 2002, Kmart filed for Chapter 11 bankruptcy protection. Two months later, Kmart shareholders filed a class-action lawsuit against CEO Chuck Conaway. Investors say they bought Kmart shares based on misleading information.

Kmart has only one patent, number 4,659,000,[*] "Carrying case for dual instruments," issued to inventors Wayne Sales and R.L. Thomasson on April 21, 1987.

So the question is: Would a more aggressive business strategy founded on the development, enforcement, and exploitation of more patents have prevented Kmart's performance from bottoming out?

Compare Kmart's patent strategy with the IP strategy of Wal-Mart, the world's largest retailer. While many question the ethics of Wal-Mart's seeming position of ignoring the patent, trade secret, trademark, trade dress, and copyright rights of others (lawsuits exist between Wal-Mart and TEVA, Tommy Hilfiger, Samara, Vanmoor, Amazon, Nike, Precise Exercise Equipment, and others), clearly Wal-Mart remains financially robust and continues to deliver increased shareholder value.

[*]A search of the U.S. Patent and Trademark Office patent database for Kmart as assignee revealed the assignment of only one patent to Kmart, although the recording of patent assignments with the USPTO is not required.

---

out your organization that a new business paradigm has been implemented and that you expect an intellectual property awareness and diligence from every employee.

Patent Awareness and Patent Management Starts at the Top

CEOs/ICOs must buy in to IP management programs if they expect senior staff to follow suit. Top-down, autocratic production structures leave little room for growth and improvement. Dr. Deming,'the father of total quality management (TQM), changed the production structure to a bottom-up style, with empowerment becoming the top-down management style. Top-down empowerment, combined with the new corporate mission statement, sets the new leadership standard for your organization.

Because PQM will be a foreign management concept to many senior staff members, it is critical that a top-down expectation be established early, that empowerment to experiment and build PQM systems is supported, and that a bottom-up PQM performance program be recognized and rewarded. (See Exhibit 12.1)

PQM is a team approach. This book introduces each functional area manager of your staff to the impact of patent management within their departments. Now, because every team needs a leader, it is time for you to step to the front and be counted. You are personally responsible to initiate this new team effort, and it may be the most important decision you will ever make as CEO of your company. Are you ready?

Intellectual Capital Officer

As the new millennium begins to mature, an increasing number of CEOs are finding it beneficial to defer executive management of intellectual property and intangible assets to a new staff member—the intellectual capital officer. What is the intellectual capital officer (ICO)?

EXHIBIT 12.1

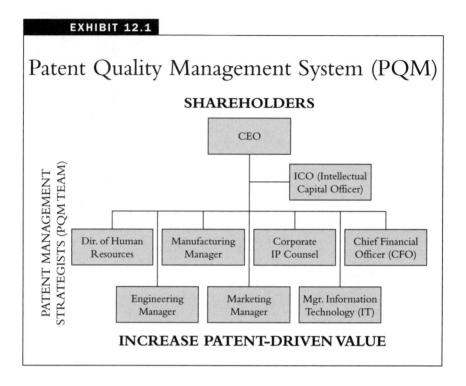

Patent Quality Management System (PQM)

SHAREHOLDERS

CEO

ICO (Intellectual Capital Officer)

PATENT MANAGEMENT STRATEGISTS (PQM TEAM)

Dir. of Human Resources

Manufacturing Manager

Corporate IP Counsel

Chief Financial Officer (CFO)

Engineering Manager

Marketing Manager

Mgr. Information Technology (IT)

INCREASE PATENT-DRIVEN VALUE

What new important and powerful role does this senior management position play in the new economy? How should the CEO or Board articulate a job description, including performance expectations and level of authority?

Because intangible assets involve patents, trademarks, trade secrets, copyrights, trade dress, employee confidentiality, facility security, and employee/competitor's espionage, internal digital security, IP litigation strategy, budgeting, and shareholder value creation, it is not unreasonable to see overall management of IP as a full-time job.

Add to this the fact that management of intellectual property and intangible assets equates to management of more than 65 percent of a given company's market cap on average, and it is clear that this is a top-level position, on par with a CEO, COO, or president, depending on corporate structure and the distribution of organizational responsibilities.

The CEO, working with corporate counsel, IP counsel, and the Board of Directors, and if required, working on approval of the shareholders, can craft a comprehensive job description for the ICO and commence recruiting efforts.

Directing the Growth of Intangible Assets

How does the CEO manage growth and development of intangible assets? It's not like managing a 5 percent production or sales increase. Rather than visualizing intellectual property management as a production line process (faster processing equals cost reduction and profits), consider IP management more of an awareness of the companywide mission of seeking out new innovation.

Intellectual asset management (IAM) is a relatively new concept in business, one that requires new tools, a new vocabulary, and a new management approach. Patent value, licensing revenues, international protection and patent investment, infringement litigation risks, competitive patent analysis, and licensing in are all components to a patent value creation program.

Such a program needs a dedicated, knowledgeable team, a strategy, and the resources to launch a tactical IP program. Once the skeleton structure of your PQM system is outlined, it's time to run it up the flagpole—pass the program around to your advisors, possibly the directors, and definitely your key staff. Now is the time to obtain buy-in to this important new program.

Establishing a PQM System

Intellectual asset management systems cannot be managed piecemeal. In order to be the least bit effective, implementation of a companywide PQM system is virtually a requirement. Such a quality system would incorporate performance metrics and periodic reporting requirements of every senior staff member, division, or cross-functional group within the enterprise.

Various management styles that have been recently popularized simply lack the focus, precision, drive, and accountability required to work with intangible corporate value components as important as patents and intellectual property. But properly launched and established, PQM can become a system that empowers managers of any style to manage their IP assets.

Establishing a PQM system in your company begins with designating a PQM steering team. From that point on, the PQM steering team takes over and outlines the company's PQM objectives in the various departments within your organization. Many of you already know how to launch a PQM system because you've recently launched a TQM system. Your PQM system follows the same team-building, performance-monitoring tenets.

So, we have laid the groundwork throughout this book for you to establish a PQM system within your organization, quickly, effectively, and efficiently. Without clear objectives, or the ability to track performance against those objectives, PQM would be little more than another slogan of the month. Although every organization will have its own objectives into which patent management can be dovetailed, we have provided an overview of some popular PQM performance metrics that you may elect to adopt, modify, and implement.

Key Initiatives
Growth Begins by Killing NIH

As they say, out with the old, in with the new. Nothing in your organization will undermine your PQM initiatives more decisively than the "not invented here" syndrome. NIH—the back-biting, territorial protectionism and egocentric management style that stifles invention and innovation—must be rooted out and destroyed before your new PQM program can take root.

There should be no sacred cows when it comes to killing NIH. CEOs simply cannot allow their managers' egos to dictate the future of the company's patent portfolio—let alone the future profitability!

Testing for NIH

How do you go about testing for the NIH syndrome? Despite the smiles and assurances that your engineering and technology development people project, often this attitude simply masks the crippling NIH problem. Rather than looking directly for the cause, look for the symptoms.

The marketing department is a good place to begin researching NIH symptoms. Because marketing professionals are on the front line and often identify features they believe are critical to product differentiation, quality, and superior performance, the marketing group often drives product design. If marketing continually meets bull-headed engineers who believe that *they* are the product developers, you've uncovered a symptom of NIH in the engineering department.

If your company has a process through which it accepts product submissions from the outside (invention submissions or idea submissions from customers), then it's time to revisit the performance of that submission process. Look for symptoms of NIH by (1) having a trusted staff member review all product submissions over the past 5 or 10 years and chart out how many of them have been accepted and adopted (acceptance ratio), and (2) compare the products submitted during the past 10 years with competitors' products that have captured market share from your company during that period. If your company turns down a submission, the product or technology can often quickly find its way to your competitor. Meeting with your PQM steering team to identify not only more NIH symptoms, but more important, programs that will eliminate NIH, can put the company in a position to begin implementing an aggressive PQM system.

Initiate the Team Effort

Kicking off a PQM program can be one of the most exciting events in building a new corporate perspective on value creation. It is a top-down initiative, but quickly breaks into a senior staff-level development effort—the structure, mission, charter, objectives, and system implementation details.

You already know how to effectively manage new systems: (1) set specific goals and objectives of what you want achieved; (2) set out a core staff to initiate the system; (3) establish performance metrics that will allow you to track the success of the system; and (4) establish a

 TIPS & TECHNIQUES

Early in its development, 3M was presented with the opportunity to acquire the rights to a new stick-tight product. A number of years later, 3M was embarrassed by the success another company was enjoying instead of themselves. Today, the product that 3M turned away from is known as Velcro.

Not to be outdone, 3M adopted one of the most aggressive programs to kill NIH, and today the company is known for its outside product submission and development programs. Thousands of new products have been brought to market since the company turned down Velcro.

Check your corporate product submission records to see whether NIH has been responsible for turning down a Velcro opportunity in your company's recent past.

rewards or recognition program that will put the spotlight on the super achievers who have excelled in meeting your objectives.

Objectives

The objectives of any PQM system are to create, grow, and protect shareholder value through the development and exploitation of intellectual property. These objectives should be reflected in the company's mission statement.

But objectives also need to be specific if managers are to have tangible targets to shoot for. These more specific objectives may include such business targets as:

- Increase market share through the acquisition of outside innovation.

- Grow revenues through the licensing of our patent portfolio to noncompetitive enterprises.

- Increase patent filings from our engineering department by XX quantity or percent.

- Foster innovation and patent development from our manufacturing group, and file at least two process patents annually.

- Introduce at least XX new proprietary products each quarter, beginning 15 months from now.

These samples are arbitrary without satisfying the overarching objectives of your company, but they show the importance of developing attainable goals for every department throughout the enterprise.

The CEO must nail down and have senior staff buy in to corporate objectives, then with the PQM steering team, develop more specific monthly, quarterly, and annual intangible assets–related goals and objectives for your departments.

Employee Recognition

Performance-based employment requires recognition for that perform-ance. How much emphasis is placed on patent recipients within the company is determined by the CEO/ICO, and the more visibility that's given to the inventors throughout the enterprise, the higher quality and more prolific the invention activity will be. Xilinx, the semiconductor company, believes so strongly in recognizing its inventors' contributions to corporate wealth that it recognizes each of them with a huge, dedi-cated space in the company—its Inventors' Hall of Fame.

This formal recognition is not inexpensive, yet the returns on this kind of investment exceed the cost and exemplify the essence of a suc-cessfully implemented PQM program.

Work with your HR managers in developing appropriate (and affordable) inventor and innovator recognition programs, and make sure these programs are effectively and continually communicated through-out the organization. Peer recognition is one of the most formidable motivation factors that drives super performance.

Metrics and Measures

It's often been said in management circles that if you can't measure it, you can't manage it. Intellectual property performance is no different. Subscribing to a continual improvement process in PQM demands that management put in place the structure to monitor and measure intel-lectual property creation development and exploitation performance.

We've outlined some possible metrics that may be valuable to your organization, but the metrics that you implement should ultimately characterize the investment your company is making in intellectual property development, any of the cost/benefit ratios that are relevant to your industry or company, and the overall increase in shareholder value attributable to your IP management processes.

Departmental and Corporate Roll-up

Just as departmental financial budgets or performance figures are rolled up into a companywide report that's presented and discussed at weekly or monthly staff meetings, so too does PQM activity need to be rolled up into CEO-level reports. The CEO/ICO can work with the staff to identify the most important intellectual property metrics for their company, meaningful information on which budget and management decisions can be made.

One of the first orders of business that the PQM Team will need to address is matching performance metrics with intellectual property management objectives. There should be participation by every key manager, from HR, manufacturing, finance, IT, legal, engineering, and finance. All managers need to find the most important metrics related to intellectual property management for their particular department, and the CEO will need to make sure that this information can be concisely reported to you on a routine basis.

But what metrics could possibly relate to IP, and how can they be characterized so they can be clearly presented and acted upon? We have outlined a few metrics that may have some level of meaning to your organization, but these metrics must be closely matched to your organization's objectives.

Intangible Asset—to—Market Value Ratio

We will start off with a finance metric. Under the new FASB-142 accounting rules, the CFO should already be moving toward monitoring and separate reporting of intangible assets. We also know that in many high-tech companies, more than 65 percent of the market value of a stock is attributable to intangible assets.

The CEO should work with the CFO in formulating a ratio that would quantify the market value, book value, and percentage of market capitalization attributable to patents and intellectual property. This ratio

259

will be more of a relative data point that will allow the CEO to track month-to-month changes rather than an absolute data point with a standalone value.

Asset Increase through Intellectual Property

Many of the metrics are little more than data already available, extracted and compiled in a reporting format. Under FASB-142, intangible assets are now being separately valued and reported. Therefore, one metric is the actual balance sheet value of the intangible assets/intellectual property. The financial assumptions underlying the reported values should be agreed to and should remain consistent with all reports.

Number of Internal Inventions/Suggestions versus Adoption Ratios

Not all metrics need to be scientific calculations. Over given periods of time, possibly monthly or quarterly, staff members can report on the number of new invention suggestions, actual invention disclosures, or number of new patents filed. These figures can originate from HR's invention suggestion box, from the product line's process improvement suggestion box, from the engineering department, or from the outside product submission program.

Is NIH alive? One way to monitor for NIH is to see whether the adoption of new ideas and inventions is improving over time. How many new suggestions have been adopted? Does this set a standard for growth and progressive thinking? If the CEO/ICOs are doing their jobs, what kind of invention adoption rates can be expected for your organization?

Number of Inventions Licensed In/Licensed Out

Here are more hard numbers that are easy to report: number of licenses, increase or decrease in current licenses, and revenue tied to the licenses.

What figures are most meaningful for your organization, and what managers will be responsible for generating those numbers. These numbers are simple, but astoundingly telling!

Make It So
Get this Book in the Hands of Your Key Managers

This book outlines the broad expectations of about every cross-functional manager within the organization. It sets the stage for you, the CEO/ICO, to carve out areas of responsibility and performance throughout the organization, with that performance emphasis being on patent quality management and increased shareholder value through intangible asset development and exploitation.

As your managers study this book, they will inherently learn what is expected of them within the corporate environment—what is expected of them by the CEO/ICO and the PQM steering team. Then, when the PQM system is launched in your company, your managers will have a clear understanding of your objectives.

Mission Statement to Include PQM

We have mentioned the importance of integrating intellectual property protection, exploitation, and increased shareholder value into your corporate mission statement. Now it's time to put this goal on your to do list.

During your next board meeting, suggest that patent and intangible asset value is so important to market cap, management objectives, and overall employee retention that the corporate mission statement should be modified to reflect the commitment the company has to IP development.

After all, from a market cap perspective, intangible assets contribute more value than the entirety of the rest of the company. Doesn't that warrant a higher visibility and commitment throughout the organization?

Delegate PQM

We could write paragraphs of information here suggesting why you need to delegate the formation of the PQM team, how to choose your founding team members, how to kick off the program, and how to manage it, but PQM boils down to one critical component: You must simply start the system.

Index of Organizations

Index